CW00502831

New Orleans

must SEES

Chief Editor	Cynthia Clayton Ochterbeck
Senior Editor	M. Linda Lee
Writer	Beth D'Addono
Production Coordinator	Allison M. Simpson
Cartography	Peter Wrenn
Photo Editor	Brigitta L. House
Documentation	Megan Thompson, Doug Rogers
Typesetting	Octavo Design and Production, Inc.
	Apopka, Florida
Cover Design	Paris Venise Design
	Paris, 17e
Printing and Binding	Quebecor World
	Laval, Québec

Contact us:

Michelin North America
One Parkway South
Greenville, SC 29615
USA
800-423-0485
www.michelin-us.com
email: TheGreenGuide-us@us.michelin.com

Special Sales:

For information regarding bulk sales, customized editions and premium sales, please contact our Customer Service Departments:

USA – 800-423-0485   **Canada** – 800-361-8236

Manufacture française des pneumatiques Michelin
Société en commandite par actions au capital de 304 000 000 EUR
Place des Carmes-Déchaux – 63 Clermont-Ferrand (France)
R.C.S. Clermont-FD B 855 800 507

© Michelin et Cie, Propriétaires-éditeurs, 2004
Dépôt légal mai 2004 – ISBN 2-06-710713-5
Printed in 04-04/1.1

Note to the reader:

While every effort is made to ensure that all information in this guide is correct and up-to-date, Michelin Travel Publications (Michelin North America, Inc.) accepts no liability for any direct, indirect or consequential losses howsoever caused so far as such can be excluded by law.

Admission prices listed for sights in this guide are for a single adult, unless otherwise specified.

Welcome to New Orleans

Table of Contents

Table of Contents

THE MICHELIN STARS

For more than 75 years, travelers have used the Michelin stars to take the guesswork out of planning a trip. Our star-rating system helps you make the best decision on where to go, what to do, and what to see. A three-star rating means it's one of the "absolutelys"; two stars means it's one of the "should sees"; and one star says it's one of the "sees" — a must if you have the time.

★★★   Absolutely Must See
★★   Really Must See
★   Must See

Three-Star Sights★★★

French Quarter★★★
Garden District★★★

Two-Star Sights★★

Acadian Cultural Center★★
Audubon Aquarium of the Americas★★
Audubon Park & Zoo★★
Bellingrath Gardens and Home★★
Cabildo★★
City Park★★
Destrehan★★
Esplanade Avenue★★
Historic New Orleans Collection★★
Jackson Square★★
Laura Plantation★★
Louisiana State Museums★★
Magazine Street★★
Presbytere★★
River Road★★
Royal Street★★
Shadows-on-the-Teche★★
St. Charles Avenue★★
St. Charles Streetcar★★
USS Alabama at Battleship Memorial Park★★

One-Star Sights★

Acadian Village★

Barataria Preserve★

Beauregard-Keyes House & Garden★

Beauvoir★

Bourbon Street★

Cajun Country★

Chalmette Battlefield and National Cemetery★

Confederate Memorial Hall★

Fairhope★

French Market★

Gallier Hall★

Gallier House★

Gulf Coast Exploreum Museum of Science★

Houmas House★

Lafayette★

Longue Vue House & Gardens★

Madewood★

Mississippi Gulf Coast★

Mobile★

Mobile Museum of Art★

Musée Conti Wax Museum★

Museum of Mobile★

National D-Day Museum★

New Orleans Museum of Art★

Nottoway Plantation★

Oak Alley★

Ocean Springs★

Ogden Museum of Southern Art★

Orpheum Theater★

Pontalba Buildings★

Preservation Hall★

San Francisco★

St. Louis Cathedral★

Vermilionville★

Warehouse Arts District★

Calendar of Events

Listed below is a selection of New Orleans' most popular annual events. Please note that dates may vary year to year. For more detailed information, contact New Orleans Metropolitan Convention & Visitor's Bureau: 800-672-6124 or www.neworleanscvb.com.

January

Battle of New Orleans
Chalmette Battlefield
504-281-0510
www.nps.gov

Sugar Bowl Classic
Louisiana Superdome
504-525-8573
www.nokiasugarbowl.com

February

Mardi Gras
Various locations
504-566-5011
www.mardigrasneworleans.com

New Orleans Boat and Sportfishing Show
Louisiana Superdome
504-780-1818
www.nmma.org

March

Literary Festival
French Quarter
www.tennesseewilliams.net

Louisiana Crawfish Festival
Frederick S. Sigur Civic Center, Chalmette
504-874-1921
www.st-bernard.la.us/tourism/LCF/lcf.htm

St. Joseph's Day Parade
French Quarter
504-561-1006

St. Patrick's Day Parade
Magazine & Race Sts.
504-455-1255

Tennessee Williams New Orleans
504-581-1144

April

Crescent City Classic 10-K Race
Starts at Jackson Square
504-861-8686
www.ccc10k.com

French Quarter Festival
French Quarter
504-522-5730
www.frenchquarterfestivals.org

New Orleans Jazz and Heritage Festival
New Orleans Fair Grounds
504-522-4786
www.nojazzfest.com

May

Greek Festival
Greek Orthodox Cathedral of the Holy Trinity, Uptown
504-282-0259
www.greekfestnola.com

New Orleans Wine and Food Experience
Various Locations
504-529-9463
www.nowfe.com

Calendar of Events

June

Great French Market Tomato Festival   504-522-2621
Decatur St., French Quarter

International Arts Festival   504-367-1313
City Park   www.internationalartsfestival.com

July

Essence Music Festival   504-566-5011
Superdome   www.neworleanscvb.com

Go 4th on the River   504-566-5011
Various locations along   www.neworleanscvb.com
the riverfront

August

Satchmo Summer Fest   504-522-5730 or 800-673-5725
Old U.S. Mint   www.satchmosummerfestival.com

Words & Music: A Literary Feast   504-586-1609
in New Orleans
Various Locations   www.wordsandmusic.org

September

Southern Decadence
French Quarter   www.southerndecadence.org

October

Art for Arts' Sake   504-528-3805
Contemporary Arts Center   www.cacno.org

Ghostly Gallivant   504-568-6968
French Quarter   www.gnofn.org

Halloween   504-566-5011
French Quarter   www.neworleanscvb.com

New Orleans Film & Video Festival   504-523-3818
Various Locations   www.neworleansfilmfest.com

Swamp Festival Audubon Zoo   504-581-4629
City Park   www.auduboninstitute.com

Voodoo Music Festival   212-379-3190
City Park   www.voodoomusicfest.com

November

Bayou Classic   504-587-3800
Superdome www.statefarm.com/sponsors/bayou.htm

Opening Day Horse Races   504-944-5515
New Orleans Fair Grounds   www.fgno.com

December

Celebration in the Oaks   504-482-4888
City Park   www.neworleanscitypark.com
Christmas in   504-522-5730 or 800-673-572
New Orleans
Various Locations   www.neworleanschristmas.com

Must Know: Practical Information

Area Codes:
Greater New Orleans area: **504**

Lafayette: **337**

North Shore: **985**

PLANNING YOUR TRIP

Before you go, contact the following organizations for information about sight-seeing, packages, hotels, restaurant reservations, recreational opportunities and special events.

New Orleans Convention and Visitors Bureau

2020 St. Charles Ave., New Orleans, LA 70130
504-566-5011; www.neworleansonline.com

For a free copy of New Orleans Good Times Guide, call 800-672-6124; to speak with a representative, call 504-566-5011; www.neworleanscvb.com.

Lafayette Convention & Visitors Commission

P.O. Box 5206, Lafayette, LA 70505
337-232-3737 or 800-346-1958; www.lafayettetravel.com

Visitor Centers

New Orleans Welcome Center

529 St. Ann St., on Jackson Square
504-568-5661
Open year-round daily 10am–5pm.
Closed Mardi Gras day & Dec 25

The center is an excellent source for maps, brochures and helpful advice.

> ### New Orleans Online
> Here are some additional Web sites to help you plan your trip:
> *www.neworleansonline.com*
> *www.neworleanscvb.com*
> *www.nola.com*
> *www.bestofneworleans.com*
> *www.bigeasy.com*

French Quarter Visitor Center of the Jean Lafitte National Historical Park

419 Decatur St.
504-589-2636; www. nps.gov/jela
Open year-round daily 9am–5pm. Closed Mardi Gras day & Dec 25.

The center offers information about the French Quarter and the six separate sites that fall under the park's administration, which include Chalmette Battlefield and Barataria Preserve.

> ### In the News
> The *Times-Picayune (www.timespicayune.com)* is the only daily newspaper in town. Its Friday entertainment section, *Lagniappe*, offers comprehensive entertainment listings. *Gambit (www.gambitweekly.com)*, a weekly tabloid, also offers information on music and entertainment; you can find a free copy at many restaurants and shops. *Offbeat (www.offbeat.com)* covers the local music industry and club scene. *The New Orleans Tribune*, which serves the African-American community, the Spanish-language *Aquí New Orleans*, and *The Jewish Civic Press* are all published monthly.

TIPS FOR SPECIAL VISITORS

Federal law requires that businesses (including hotels and restaurants) provide access for the disabled, devices for the hearing impaired, and designated parking spaces. For further information, contact the Society for Accessible Travel and Hospitality (SATH), 347 Fifth Ave., Suite 610, New York NY 10016 *(212-447-7284; www.sath.org).*

All national parks have facilities for the disabled, and offer free or discounted passes. For details, contact the National Park Service *(Office of Public Inquiries, P.O. Box 37127, Room 1013, Washington, DC 20013-7127; 202-208-4747; www.nps.gov).*

Passengers who will need assistance with train or bus travel should give advance notice to Amtrak *(800-872-7245 or 800-523-6590/TDD; www.amtrak.com)* or Greyhound *(800-752-4841 or 800-345-3109/TDD; www.greyhound.com).* Reservations for hand-controlled rental cars should be made in advance with the rental company.

Local Lowdown – The following publications provide detailed information about access for the disabled in New Orleans:

- **Advocacy Center for the Elderly and Disabled** *(504-522-2337 or 800-960-7705 voice or TDD; www.icdri.org/legal/LouisianaPAD.htm)*
- **Easter Seal Society of Louisiana for Children and Adults with Disabilities** *(504-523-7325 voice or TDD; 800-695-7325)*
- **LIFT** provides information about specialized transportation systems *(504-827-7433)*
- **Louisiana Commission for the Deaf** *(800-543-2099 or 800-543-2099/TDD)*
- **Louisiana Relay Service** *(800-947-5277 or 800-846-5266/TDD)*

Senior Citizens – Many hotels, attractions and restaurants offer discounts to visitors age 62 or older (proof of age may be required). The **American Association of Retired Persons** (AARP), *(601 E St. NW, Washington DC 20049; 202-424-3410; www.aarp.com)* offers discounts to its members.

Important Phone Numbers	
Emergency 24hrs (police/fire/ambulance)	911
Police (non-emergency)	504-565-7530
Medical Emergencies	
House Calls USA	800-468-3537
Tulane University Professional Physician's Referral Group	504-588-5800
New Orleans Dental Association (referrals)	504-834-6449
24-hour Pharmacies:	
Rite Aid, 2 locations in New Orleans *(www.riteaid.com):*	
3401 St. Charles Ave., Garden District	504-896-4575
3100 Gentilly Blvd., Mid-City	504-940-1480
Poison Control	800-256-9822
Traveler's Aid Society	504-525-8726
Time & Weather (fee)	504-828-4000

Must Know: Practical Information

WHEN TO GO

New Orleans is a steamy place, with humidity a factor year-round. In winter months temperatures can fluctuate wildly, from 40 to 75 degrees, so pack layers just in case. Summers can be oppressive with high humidity and temperatures soaring into the 90s. Summer is also hurricane season, which runs from the beginning of June to the end of November, with most of the tropical activity occurring in August and September. Spring (April & May) and fall (October & November), when it's cooler, are the best times to visit.

New Orleans Average Seasonal Temperatures

	Jan	Apr	July	Oct
Avg. High	63°F / 17°C	79°F / 26°C	91°F / 33°F	79°F / 26°C
Avg. Low	43°F / 6°C	59°F / 15°C	73°F / 23°C	59°F / 15°C

GETTING THERE

By Air – New Orleans is serviced by **Louis Armstrong New Orleans International Airport** (**MSY**) located in the suburb of Kenner, about 11mi west of downtown New Orleans *(504-464-0831; www.flymsy.com)*. A cab ride from the airport to the Central Business District costs about $28.

By Train – Service to **Union Station** *(1001 Loyola Ave.)* in New Orleans is provided by Amtrak *(800-872-7245; www.amtrak.com)*. Amtrak's Coastliner runs to the Gulf Coast and many other places along the route.

By Bus – Greyhound provides service to and from Union Station in New Orleans *(1001 Loyola Ave.)*. For schedules and fares, contact Greyhound *(504-524-7571 or 800-229-9424; www.greyhound.com)*.

By Car – To get to New Orleans, I-10 provides highway access from the east and west. From the north, take I-55 South to the city. US-61 runs north to Baton Rouge.

Car Rental Companies

Car Rental Company	Reservations	Internet
Alamo	800-327-9633	www.alamo.com
Avis	800-331-1212	www.avis.com
Budget	800-527-0700	www.drivebudget.com
Enterprise	800-736-8222	www.enterprise.com
Hertz	800-654-3131	www.hertz.com
National	800-227-7368	www.nationalcar.com
Thrifty	800-367-2277	www.thrifty.com

GETTING AROUND

By Car – Considering that New Orleans is also the town with drive-through Daiquiri Huts, it's best to remember that the local police take the rules of the road very seriously, which includes mandatory use of seat belts and enforcement of speed limits, especially on the airport approach roads. You'll notice that traffic lights blink after dark in some neighborhoods; this is a signal to slow down and check for other cars in the intersection before continuing on your way.

Parking – Finding street parking in the French Quarter and the Central Business District is a challenge, and parking rules are strictly enforced. Never park within 3ft of a private driveway. Canal Place Parking Garage *(365 Canal St.; 504 522-9200)* is conveniently located near riverfront attractions and the French Quarter. Call **Central Parking Corporation** for more information *(504-525-3191; www.parking.com)*. If you think your car has been towed, call the Claiborne Auto Pound *(400 N. Claiborne Ave. at Conti St.; 504-565-7450)*. Be prepared to identify your vehicle by license number, make, color, and former parking location.

> ### Driving in the French Quarter
>
> If you're driving in the Quarter, remember that Royal Street is closed to cars between Jackson Square and Canal Street from 11am–5pm. Bourbon Street closes to vehicles between Canal Street and St. Peter Street every evening from 6pm–7am.

By Foot – New Orleans is a very walkable city, particularly in the French Quarter, with its easy grid of streets. Like any other city, New Orleans can be unsafe for tourists who don't keep their wits about them. Pickpockets can prey on inebriated tourists on Bourbon Street, so stay alert. At night, it's best to travel in groups and stay in well-lighted areas with plenty of pedestrian traffic. Streets above Bourbon towards Rampart can be dicey—if in doubt, take a cab.

By Public Transportation – The **New Orleans Regional Transit Authority** (**NORTA**) runs an extensive network of buses and streetcars throughout the metropolitan area. Call NORTA's 24-hour **RideLine** *(504-827-7802; www.regionaltransit.org)* for route and fare information.

Buses and Streetcars – **Bus** routes, both local and express, are extensive and most routes run daily around the clock. The fare is $1.25 and transfers are 10 cents; express bus fare is $1.50 *(exact change required)*. **Streetcars**, including the **St. Charles Avenue Streetcar**★★ *(see Musts for Fun)*, operate daily around the clock; the fare is $1.25.

Consider purchasing an RTA **VisiTour Pass,** which is available for either one day *($5)* or three consecutive days *($12)* of unlimited travel on all forms of public transportation. Passes are sold at information counters in many hotels and shops (look for the RTA sticker in the window).

By Ferry – *Canal Street Landing is located at Riverwalk Marketplace. 800-445-4109. www.neworleanspaddlewheels.com.* You can cross the Mississippi River to Algiers daily except on Christmas Day (Dec 25). Boats leave the Canal Street dock every half-hour beginning at 6am, with the last round-trip leaving from Canal Street at 11:30pm and returning at 1:45pm. Pedestrians ride free; cars pay $1 for the return trip from Algiers.

> ### Navigating New Orleans
>
> Sitting as it does on the bend of the Mississippi River, New Orleans has earned the nickname the "Crescent City." This unusual shape often causes confusion when you're trying to find your way around the city, as the cardinal directions—north, south, east and west—don't apply. Directions in the Big Easy are given in terms of uptown (upriver toward the Garden District and beyond), downtown (beginning in the Central Business District and extending through the French Quarter), lakebound (toward Lake Pontchartrain) and riverbound (toward the Mississippi River).

Must Know: Practical Information

Taxis – **United Cabs** *(504-522-9771)*, **Checker-Yellow Cabs** *(504-486-9967)*, or **White Fleet Cabs** *(504-948-6635)* are the most common rides in town. Be sure the meter is turned on, and remember that a flat fare of $3 per passenger (or the regular meter rate, if it's greater) is in effect during special events, such as Mardi Gras and Jazz Fest, Bowl games and Saints home games. Any questions of problems, call the **Taxicab Bureau** *(504-565-6272)*.

FOREIGN VISITORS

Visitors from outside the US can obtain information from the New Orleans Convention and Visitors Bureau *(504-566-5011; www.neworleansonline.com)* or from the US embassy or consulate in their country of residence. There are a number of foreign embassies and consulates located in New Orleans; for a listing, check online at: *www.wtcno.org/tradinfo/consularcorps.htm*. For a complete list of American consulates and embassies abroad, visit the US State Department Bureau of Consular Affairs listing on the Internet at: *http://travel.state.gov/links.html*.

Entry Requirements – Travelers entering the United States under the Visa Waiver Program (VWP) must have a machine-readable passport. Any traveler without a machine-readable passport will be required to obtain a visa before entering the US. Citizens of VWP countries are permitted to enter the US for general business or tourist purposes for a maximum of 90 days without needing a visa. Requirements for the Visa Waiver Program can be found at the Department of State's Visa Services Web site *(http://travel.state.gov/vwp.html)*.

All citizens of non-participating countries must have a visitor's visa. Upon entry, nonresident foreign visitors must present a valid passport and a round-trip transportation ticket. Canadian citizens are not required to present a passport or visa, but they must present a valid picture ID and proof of citizenship. Naturalized Canadian citizens should carry their citizenship papers.

US Customs – All articles brought into the US must be declared at the time of entry. Prohibited items: plant material; firearms and ammunition (if not for sporting purposes); meat or poultry products. For information, contact the US Customs Service, 1300 Pennsylvania Ave. NW, Washington DC 20229 *(202-354-1000; www.cbp.gov)*.

Money and Currency Exchange – Visitors can exchange currency at these locations in the Central Business District: **American Express** *(201 St. Charles Ave.; 504-586-8201)*; **First National Bank of Commerce** *(210 Baronne St.; 504-561-1371)*; or the **Whitney National Bank** *(228 St. Charles Ave.; 504-586-7272)*. Banks are generally open Mon–Fri, 9am–3pm. Automated teller machines (ATMs) are located throughout the city.

For cash transfers, **Western Union** *(800-325-6000; www.westernunion.com)* has agents throughout the city. Banks, stores, restaurants and hotels accept travelers' checks with picture identification. To report a lost or stolen credit card: **American Express** *(800-528-4800)*; **Diners Club** *(800-234-6377)*; **MasterCard** *(800-307-7309)*; **Visa** *(800-336-8472)*.

Driving in the US – Visitors bearing a valid driver's license issued by their country of residence are not required to obtain an International Driver's License. Drivers must carry vehicle registration and/or rental contract, and proof of automobile insurance at all times. Gasoline is sold by the gallon (1 gal=3.8 liters). Vehicles in the US are driven on the right-hand side of the road.

Electricity – Voltage in the US is 120 volts AC, 60 Hz. Foreign-made appliances may need AC adapters (available at specialty travel and electronics stores) and North American flat-blade plugs.

Taxes and Tipping – Prices displayed in the US do not includes sales tax (9% in New Orleans Parish). An amusement tax (which includes sales tax) adds up to 14 percent for concert and theater tickets and for cover charges in bars with live music.

It is customary to give a small gift of money—a **tip**—for services rendered to waiters 15–20% of the bill), porters ($1 per bag), chamber maids ($1 per day), and cab drivers (15% of fare). If your hotel concierge has provided exceptional service, $5 is a standard tip.

Louisiana Tax Free

Shopping is designed to promote international tourism in Louisiana by giving a refund on sales taxes at participating merchants. The tax applies to those who can show a foreign passport and an international travel ticket, and who will be in the country for less than 90 days. All shops in the airport, as well as selected businesses throughout the city, offer tax-free shopping. You can get detailed information about refunds at the Tax Free Counter located on the upper level of the airport's main terminal *(504-467-0723; open year-round daily 7am–6pm daily; closed except Mardi Gras day & Dec 25)*.

Time Zone – New Orleans is located in the Central Time zone, six hours behind Greenwich Mean Time, and one hour behind New York City.

Measurement Equivalents

Degrees Fahrenheit	95°	86°	77°	68°	59°	50°	41°	32°	23°	14°
Degrees Celsius	35°	30°	25°	20°	15°	10°	5°	0°	-5°	-10°

1 inch = 2.5 centimeters   1 foot = 30.48 centimeters
1 mile = 1.6 kilometers   1 pound = 0.45 kilograms
1 quart = 0.9 liters   1 gallon = 3.78 liters

Where y'at?

Those locals definitely have their own lingo. Here's a primer to get you going:

Gras-doux (grah-DOO) – Unpleasant grime or detritus (don't look down at that gras-doux on Bourbon Street).

Gris-gris (gree-gree) – A voodoo hex or charm.

Krewe – The private clubs that organize and participate in Mardi Gras parades.

Lagniappe – (LAN-yap) A little something extra given away in the spirit of good will. It's also the name of the weekend section of the local paper, the *Times-Picayune*.

Making groceries – What a native New Orleanian says when he's going grocery shopping.

Where y'at? – How's it going?

Must Know: Practical Information

ACCOMMODATIONS

For a list of suggested accommodations, see Must Stay.

Reservation Services:

Crescent City.com – 800-368-4876; www.crescentcity.com.

New Orleans Hotel Hotline – 800-361-1029; http://neworleans.hotel-hotline.com.

JazzNet Hotels – 888-763-0753; www.jazznethotels.com.

Hostels – *www.hostelneworleans.com.* A no-frills, inexpensive alternative to hotels, hostels are a great choice for budget travelers. Prices average $25–$75 per night.

Campgrounds – New Orleans West KOA *(504-467-1792 or 800-562-5110).*

Major hotel and motel chains with locations in New Orleans include:

Property	Phone	Web site
Best Western	800-535-7862	www.bestwestern.com
Courtyard By Marriott	800-321-2211	www.marriott.com
Days Inn	800 242-1945	www.daysinn.com
Doubletree	800-222-8733	www.doubletree.com
Embassy Suites	800-362-2779	www.embassysuites.com
Hampton Inn	800-292-0653	www.hamptoninn.com
Hilton	800-445-8667	www.hilton.com
Holiday Inn	800-535-7830	www.holiday-inn.com
Hyatt	800-233-1234	www.hyatt.com
La Quinta Inn	800-531-5900	www.lq.com
Marriott	800 654-3990	www.marriott.com
Omni	800-843-6664	www.omnihotels.com
Radisson	800-333-3333	www.radisson.com
Ramada Inn	800-535-9141	www.ramada.com
Ritz-Carlton	800-241-3333	www.ritzcarlton.com
Sheraton	800-235-3396	www.Sheraton.com

SPORTS

New Orleans is known for hosting college bowl and Superbowl games, but its professional sports teams also draw a loyal following.

Sport/Team	Season	Venue	Phone	Web site
NFL Football/ New Orleans Saints	Sept–Dec	Superdome	504-731-1700	www.neworleanssaints.com
AFL Football/New Orleans Voodoo	Sept–Dec	New Orleans Arena	504-731-1700	www.govoodoo.com
NBA Basketball/New Orleans Hornets	Oct–Apr	New Orleans Arena	504-301-4000	www.nba.com/hornets
AAA Baseball/New Orleans Zephyrs	Apr–Oct	Zephyr Field	504-734-5155	www.zephyrsbaseball.com

Gay & Lesbian New Orleans

There is a large and visible gay and lesbian population in New Orleans, with an extensive network of support and hospitality services available to gay visitors. There are gay bars and discos, gay-owned hotels and guesthouses and come Mardi Gras, gay krewes that throw some of the best parties in town.

For general information, stop by or call the Lesbian and Gay Community Center *(2114 Decatur St.; 504-945-1103; www.lgccno.org)*. The best resources for entertainment and news is *Ambush Magazine (www.ambushmag.com)* and *Impact Gulf South Gay News*, both of which serve the gay, lesbian, bisexual, and transgender communities. Before your visit, check out www.gayneworleans.com, a helpful site that offers information on everything from accommodations to restaurants, arts and culture and, of course, nightlife.

New Orleans

Let the Good Times Roll: New Orleans

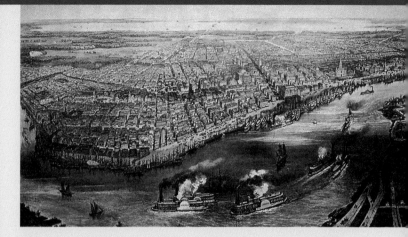

If they know one thing in New Orleans, they know how to party. Why, the city's free-wheeling melting pot of French, Spanish, English, Africans, West Indians and others have been mixing it up since 1718 when Jean Baptiste Le Moyne first laid claim to La Nouvelle Orleans for France. Theirs is a sultry city where the pace of life is slower than most and the temptation to overindulge—be it in food, drink or just having too much fun—is great. In New Orleans, they're serious when they say "laissez les bons temps rouler" (let the good times roll).

The site French explorer Jean-Baptiste Le Moyne chose atop a raised embankment along the Mississippi River was strategically important as the gateway to the Louisiana Territory, but it proved equally inauspicious for settlement. Colonists battled hurricanes, floods, fire, and mosquito-born epidemics of yellow fever and malaria as they struggled to exist in the muddy low-lying outpost now known as the French Quarter. In 1769 the city came under Spanish rule, but it was returned to France in 1803.

A month later, in what may have been the real-estate deal of all time, Napoleon sold the 830,000sq mi Louisiana Territory to the US on April 30, 1803 for $15 million—or about four cents an acre. Through the **Louisiana Purchase,** the US gained what eventually became all or part of 15 states, and inherited the thriving port of New Orleans, a city unlike any other in America, both then and now.

Cajun vs. Creole

You'll hear these two terms a lot while you're in town. They're used to describe the people as well as the culinary heritage from two unique cultures. But what's the difference between the two?

The name given to European colonists and their descendants in the fledgling settlement of New Orleans, the term Creole grew to encompass the African and Caribbean peoples who were brought here via the slave trade or who came following the Haitian Revolution in the early 19C. Deported from Acadia (now Nova Scotia) in 1755 for refusing to swear allegiance to the British Crown, fervently Catholic Acadian traders and farmers—or Cajuns—settled in the swamps and bayous outside of town. This exotic stew of cultures has left an indelible stamp on the city's architecture, cuisine, language and general sense of laissez-faire.

Let the Good Times Roll: New Orleans

In the decades following the Louisiana Purchase, settlers flooded west to occupy the new territory. By 1840, New Orleans ranked as the fourth-largest city in the US, its prosperity buoyed by a rich river trade in cotton and tobacco. Despite the city's unification under the American flag, New Orleans was not a unified society. Americans, who found themselves unwelcome in the French Quarter by the Creoles, settled on the other side of Canal Street, which became the "neutral ground" between the two feuding groups.

In the early 20C (1897–1917), the steamy clubs and bordellos in the red-light district of Storyville gave birth to a new genre of uniquely American music—jazz. It was here that greats Louis Armstrong, Buddy Bolden and Jelly Roll Morton all got their start.

Economic prosperity flowed with the discovery of oil beneath the Gulf of Mexico in 1901. Over the next two decades, refineries mushroomed along the Mississippi between Baton Rouge and New Orleans. Today oil remains the number-one industry in town, and New Orleans reigns as the country's largest port, with 5,000 ships from 60 different countries docking here each year.

Despite the sweltering weather in summer, New Orleans has become a year-round destination. The city, whose multicultural vibe resists homogenization to this day, is still plagued by occasional hurricanes and floods, but it just keeps rolling along. And those who love New Orleans like an eccentric family member wouldn't have it any other way.

Fast Facts
• New Orleans Metro Area covers 360 square miles—200sq mi of land and 160sq mi of water.
• The city's population numbers 600,000 people
• New Orleans boasts 35,000 buildings on the National Register of Historic Places; that's more than in Washington, DC.
• Each year, some 7.9 million visitors spend $4.5 billion in the Big Easy.
• In 2003, 2.3 million Mardi Gras revelers generated some 1,900 tons of trash.

From the renowned French Quarter and the residential Garden District to tiny Tremé, New Orleans' soul lies in its neighborhoods. Don't miss out on exploring these distinctly different districts.

French Quarter★★★

Bounded by the Mississippi River, Rampart & Canal Sts. & Esplanade Ave. www.frenchquarter.com.

With its Old World spirit and its infinitely varied architecture, the French Quarter is truly a place like no other. From the sounds of jazz wafting on the sultry air down Bourbon Street to the the cayenne-flavored cuisine, the French Quarter offers unforgettable experiences to the traveler with an open heart and a healthy appetite for the fantastic.

Founded in 1718 as a walled military outpost on the bend of the Mississippi River, the Quarter was a rich tapestry of French, Spanish and African cultures that combined to create a hybrid personality all its own. The passing of three centuries has seen the area ravaged by fires, floods, misguided development and benign neglect, yet through it all, the Vieux Carré—as the French called it (locals say VOO cuh-RAY)—has never lost its identity or its Bohemian soul.

In a world where theme parks re-create history for the masses, the French Quarter is unfailingly authentic; it is 120 blocks of narrow streets and shuttered Creole cottages, with more than 35,000 buildings listed on the National Register of Historic Places.

Make Mine a Muffuletta

Philadelphia has its hoagie, New York has its sub sandwich, and New Orleans has its muffuletta, a savory, Dagwood-sized layering of Italian meats and cheeses slathered with spicy olive salad and stacked between thick slices of Sicilian bread. **Central Grocery** *(923 Decatur St.; 504-523-1620; see Must Eat)* is the place to try one of these local specialties, which aren't for the faint of appetite.

Best Streets of the French Quarter

Around every bend in the Vieux Carré, you're bound to find a lovely hidden courtyard garden or some remnant of history.

Royal Street★★

Royal St. is closed to vehicles from Jackson Square to Canal Street daily 10am–6pm.

Best known for its 10 blocks of antique shops and art galleries *(see Must Shop)*, Royal Street is also the address of some of the Quarter's most elegant homes, many of which have been lived in by the same families for generations. The street attracts musicians and tarot-card readers to add to its entertainment allure.

Gallier House★ *– 1118-1132 Royal St. See Historic Sites.*

Bourbon Street★

Bourbon St. is closed to vehicles between Canal St. & St. Peter St. daily, 6pm–7am.

Locals may avoid it like the plague, but you have to experience it for yourself—preferably at night. Lights flash, music booms and hawkers stand in doorways beckoning the uninitiated to the dubious wanton pleasures within. Bourbon Street is unquestionably tasteless, with its tacky souvenir shops, strip joints, rows of bars and stumbling drunks. But despite what you see, there is good music here, from Dixieland to blues and zydeco. Think of it as the ultimate reality-TV show, and jump right in.

Chartres Street

This thoroughfare's mix of residential and shopping includes historic architecture, such as the **Pontalba Buildings**★ at Jackson Square *(see Historic Sights)* and the **Pharmacy Museum,** the nation's first licensed drug store *(see Museums)*. Shops stock a range of items from funky antiques to discount clothing and novel accessories for the home.

Decatur Street

Once the Quarter's roughest piece of riverfront real estate, Decatur Street at Canal has been somewhat gentrified, thanks to Canal Place and Jax Brewery shopping malls *(see Must Shop)* and chains like House of Blues, Hard Rock Café and Virgin Megastore. Shop at the latter if you must, but for hard-to-find local music you're better off at the **Louisiana Music Factory** *(210 Decatur St.; see Must Shop)*.

Decatur Street at **Jackson Square**★★ is the Quarter's prime tourist area, the place to climb aboard a horse-drawn carriage *(see Musts for Fun)*, have your palm read and line up for photo ops with **St. Louis Cathedral**★ in the background. A bit further down, you'll find the **French Market**★ and **Café du Monde**, de rigueur for café au lait and beignets *(see Musts for Fun)*. At the corner of Decatur and Esplanade, visit the **U.S. Mint** with its historic jazz exhibit *(see Museums)*.

The Rest of the French Quarter's Best

Audubon Aquarium of the Americas★★ – *Foot of Canal St. on the riverfront. See Musts for Kids.*

Cabildo★★ – *On Jackson Square. See Museums.*

Historic New Orleans Collection★★ – *533 Royal St. See Museums.*

Jackson Square★★ – *Decatur St. between St. Peter & St. Ann Sts. See Historic Sites.*

Presbytère★★ – *Jackson Square. See Museums.*

Beauregard-Keyes House★ – *1113 Chartres St. See Historic Sites.*

French Market★ – *Decatur St. between St. Ann & Barracks Sts. See Must Shop.*

Gallier House★ – *1132 Royal St. See Historic Sites.*

Musée Conti Wax Museum★ – *917 Conti St. See Museums.*

Pontalba Buildings★ – *Jackson Square. See Historic Sites.*

Preservation Hall★ – *726 St. Peter St. See Nightlife.*

St. Louis Cathedral★ – *On Jackson Square. See Historic Sites.*

A Streetcar Named Desire

Sure, it's a well-known play by one-time New Orleans resident Tennessee Williams, and, later, a movie starring Marlin Brando (who can forget his bellows of "Stella!"?). But the streetcar named Desire did actually travel along Royal and Bourbon streets until 1948. It was replaced by a bus named Desire, which somehow just doesn't have the same ring to it.

Garden District★★★

Bounded by Jackson & Louisiana Aves. and Magazine Street & St. Charles Ave.

A walk through the Garden District in one of the great pleasures of visiting New Orleans. Like much of the city, the Garden District was originally the site of a plantation, but unlike the French Quarter and Faubourg Marigny that retained their French and Creole roots, the Garden District was distinctly American.

Originally called Lafayette, the neighborhood was settled by wealthy Americans in the early 19C, when a combination of Mississippi River commerce, regional cash crops, and the slave trade created more than a few millionaires in need of uptown digs. A culture clash between the newcomers and the well-established French Creoles created a literal dividing line—Canal Street—between the two groups.

In the Garden District, Americans built homes that were as far away from the French and Creole style as possible, hence the Victorian, Italianate and Greek Revival-style residences that still line the streets and draw for tourists in search of notable architecture. Prytania Street and the numbered streets leading from it to Magazine Street make for delightful wandering.

Magazine Street★★

This street is the Garden District's answer to hip Melrose Avenue in Los Angeles *(see Michelin Must Sees Los Angeles)*. A working-class area that runs between the Mississippi River and St. Charles Avenue, Magazine Street is filled with funky shops and cool cafes and bars *(see Must Shop)*.

St. Charles Avenue★★

Even if you're not a student of architecture, you're bound to appreciate the beauty of the antebellum and Victorian mansions that line this lovely, wide thoroughfare. Enormous live oak trees that overhang the avenue add to the sense of romance.

One of the best ways to see the Garden District is to take the **St. Charles Avenue streetcar**★★ *(see Musts for Fun)* from Canal Street all the way up to Carrollton Avenue. When you see something that looks interesting, just hop off and investigate. The street is dotted with huge antebellum mansions and hotels.

Garden District Highlights

Here are a few noteworthy homes to include on your walking tour of the Garden District—please respect that these are private residences (with the exception of Commander's Palace restaurant) and are not open to the public.

Bradish Johnson House and Louise S. McGehee School — *2343 Prytania St.* Sugar magnate Bradish Johnson spent $100,000—close to $1.5 million today—to build this Second Empire-style mansion in 1872. Since 1929, the building has been the private Louise S. McGehee School for girls.

Commander's Palace — *1403 Washington Ave.* Established in 1883 by Emile Commander, this turreted Victorian structure is the jewel in the Brennan family restaurant crown, perennially ranked among the nation's top eateries *(see Must Eat)*.

Robinson House — *1415 Third St.* Architect Henry Howard built this striking mansion between 1859 and 1865 for tobacco merchant Walter Robinson. Thanks to water collected on the roof, and carried by gravity into the home's water closets, its residents enjoyed an early form of indoor plumbing.

Toby's Corner — *2340 Prytania St.* Thought to be the oldest home in the Garden District, this Greek Revival mansion was built in 1838 for Philadelphia wheelwright Thomas Toby.

Anne Rice

Queen of gothic prose, New Orleans native Anne Rice attracts legions of tourists who line up to see her home, or at least its front gate, in the Garden District at 1239 First Street *(at Chestnut St.)*. Her vampire series, which began with *Interview with a Vampire* in 1976, conjures up an unabashedly romantic view of New Orleans at its decadent best. Here are a few Anne Rice landmarks, in case you're planning a pilgrimage to her Garden District neighborhood.

2301 St. Charles Avenue — Anne Rice's childhood home.

Garden District Book Shop — *2727 Prytania St.* Built in 1884 as the Crescent City Skating Rink, this building knew many incarnations before it became Anne Rice's favorite bookstore. She always holds her first book signing here when a new book is released, and the shop stocks a supply of pricey signed first editions for her most rabid fans.

Rosegate — *1239 First St.* This is Rice's primary residence, which she used to open to the public for tours and for a Halloween bash every year—a practice she stopped when her husband, Stan, died a few years ago. Called Rosegate for the rosette pattern on the fence, this house is the setting for her *Witching Hour* series.

Warehouse Arts District ★

Bounded by Baronne St., Erato St., Convention Center Blvd. & Lafayette St.

Once storage central for the massive quantities of cotton, sugar and coffee that were shipped from the port of New Orleans, this district lost its sense of purpose as the city's shipping operations moved farther upriver. By the 1970s into the early 1980s as the wharves were torn down to make way for riverfront development, this area of abandoned warehouses became a no-man's land of crumbling industrial buildings.

Galleries began creeping slowly into the downtown backwater after the founding of the Contemporary Arts Center in 1976. The 1984 Louisiana World's Fair further called attention to the neighborhood, which was ripe for development. Soon 19C warehouses were being transformed into lofts, offices and galleries, and Emeril Lagasse's namesake restaurant on Tchoupitoulas Street *(see Must Eat)*, led the way for other upscale eateries. Today the Warehouse Arts District shines as the hub of the arts and culture scene in New Orleans, with art galleries clustered along **Julia Street** *(see sidebar below)*.

Confederate Memorial Hall ★ – *929 Camp St. See Museums.*

National D-Day Museum ★ – *945 Magazine St. See Museums.*

Ogden Museum of Southern Art ★ – *925 Camp St. See Museums.*

Contemporary Arts Center – *900 Camp St. See Museums.*

Louisiana Children's Museum – *420 Julia St. See Musts for Kids.*

Gallery Row

Julia Street between Camp Street and Tchoupitoulas Street is the place to shop for cutting-edge contemporary art in New Orleans. Anchored by the innovative Contemporary Arts Center on Camp Street, this swath of the neighborhood showcases some of the region's finest artists, at their grittiest and most passionate. Here's a sampling of what you'll find:

- **LeMieux Gallery** *(332 Julia St.; 504-522-5988; www.lemieuxgalleries.com)* presents "Third Coast art," work by Gulf Coast artists from Louisiana to Florida. Here you'll find canvases by Paul Ninas, an early New Orleans Modernist known for his moody French Quarter renderings.

- **Arthur Roger Gallery** *(432 Julia St.; 504-522-1999; www.arthurrogergallery.com)* is a leader in both regional and national contemporary art, with works by Paul Cadmus and Mary Jane Parker, among others.

- **Ariodante Contemporary Craft Gallery** *(535 Julia St.; 504-524-3233)* features upscale crafts at approachable prices.

- **George Schmidt** *(626 Julia St.; 504-592-0206; www.georgeschmidt.com)* presents lively canvases that the gallery's namesake describes as "history painting, narrative art and other reactionary work on paper and canvas."

- **Marguerite Oestreicher Fine Arts** *(720 Julia St.; 504-581-9253)*, located in a former carriage house, mines the globe for an international selection of 20C paintings, prints and sculptures.

Central Business District

Bounded by Canal St., the Mississippi, I-10 and the Ponchartrain Expressway.

A mix of luxury hotels and modern development, the Central Business District (CBD) was known as Faubourg Sainte-Marie when Americans began settling here after the Louisiana Purchase. The American community revolved around Lafayette Square, site of **Gallier Hall**★ *(see Landmarks)*, which served as the city hall at the time. Canal Street, an impressive 171ft wide, was the neutral ground that separated the often fractious French and American communities. It's in the CBD that you'll find the city's skyscrapers, sports arenas and the hub of the local legal community, along with the **Riverwalk Marketplace** *(see Must Shop)* and Harrah's casino.

Harrah's New Orleans Casino – *On the riverfront at Canal St. between Pl. de France & St. Peters St. 504-533-6000 or 800-847-5299. www.harrahsneworleans.com.* Feeling lucky? Then you'll want to go by Harrah's. Opened in 2000, this Greek Revival gambling palace offers more than 2,500 slot machines and 10 varieties of gaming tables, from Baccarat to poker—all available 24 hours a day.

Coffee in the Crescent City

Bet you didn't know that coffee first came to America by way of New Orleans back in the mid 1700's. It's true—the French brought coffee with them from Martinique as they began to settle new colonies along the Mississippi. During the Civil War, when coffee was hard to come by, New Orleans' French citizens began adding chicory to stretch their precious coffee grounds. Chicory is the root of the endive plant, which, when roasted and ground, softens the bitter edge of dark-roasted coffee and imbues the beverage with an chocolatey flavor. Chicory-blended coffee is brewed at all the best coffee houses in town, usually served as café au lait, with hot milk added.

Try these java joints when you need a pick-me-up:

• **C C's Coffee House** – *650 Poydras St., French Quarter. 504-586-0278.*

• **Fair Grinds** – *3133 Ponce de Leon St., Mid-City. 504-948-3222.*

• **House of Brews New Orleans** – *933 Royal St., French Quarter. 504-525-0333.*

• **Neutral Ground Coffee House** – *5110 Danneel St., Uptown. 504-891-3381.*

Faubourg Marigny

Bounded by Esplanade & Elysian Fields Aves., the Mississippi River and Rampart St.

This Creole neighborhood on the east edge of the French Quarter was named for 18C aristocrat and good-time guy Bernard de Marigny de Mandeville, who at the tender age of 15 inherited the plantation that once defined the district. In 1806, thanks to his mounting gambling debts, Marigny began to sell off parcels of land at a good price to "les hommes de couleur libres" (free men of color) instead of to American developers. Thus New Orleans' first suburb (*faubourg* in French) was born.

In the past decade, the Marigny has emerged as one of the hottest spots in town, home to dozens of nightclubs and restaurants. Bohemian Marigny is a great place to check out where, and how, a colorful segment of locals live. **Frenchmen Street**, the Marigny's main artery, is chockablock with cafes, book-stores and clubs, including Snug Harbor, Café Brasil, d.b.a. and the Spotted Cat *(see Nightlife)*. Younger urban dwellers have moved into the area in droves recently, contributing to what has become the busiest real-estate market in New Orleans. Along with the adjacent sections of the French Quarter, the Marigny is also the social center for the city's gay and lesbian communities.

Shotgun Houses

Found in many New Orleans neighborhoods, especially in Faubourg Marigny, Mid-City and the Irish Channel, shotgun houses served as cheap housing for laborers and made good use of narrow lots. Typically one-room wide (the style was later modified into an L shape), the shotgun house with its long row of back-to-back rooms probably evolved on Haitian sugar plantations. It was said that if you were to fire a gun through the front door of one of these structures, the bullet would pass straight through the line of rooms and go right out the back. The open design of these houses also keeps the air circulating, making it ideal for the Crescent City's humid summer climate.

Mid-City

Bounded by Robert E. Lee Blvd., St. Bernard Ave., Canal Blvd. & I-10

Mid-City encompasses a colorful swath of neighborhoods, including residential Esplanade Ridge on either side of **Esplanade Avenue**★, and the city's historic racetrack, **Fair Grounds Race Course** *(1751 Gentilly Blvd.)*. In the 19C, Esplanade was the grand avenue of New Orleans' Creole society—the St. Charles Avenue for people of color. Although many sections of the avenue have gone downhill, there are still stately mansions here that date back to the 19C, some of which have been turned into inns and B&Bs. If you're in the neighborhood, don't miss a visit to Rock-N-Bowl *(see Nightlife)*.

City Park★★ – *North end of Esplanade Ave. See Parks and Gardens, and Musts for Kids.*

New Orleans Museum of Art★ – *In City Park. See Museums.*

Tremé

Bounded by Canal St., I-10, Esplanade Ave. & Rampart St.

The oldest African-American settlement in the US, Tremé (say: tre-MAY) Historical District also ranks as the first neighborhood where free people of color were able to own their own homes during an era when America was mired in slavery. In 1898 the district took a dramatic turn when the city took a section of Tremé and named it **Storyville** in an attempt to curtail prostitution. Storyville, with its wild mix of brothels, bars, lax liquor laws, monied plantation-owner patrons, and musicians, created the perfect recipe for jazz music. Tremé was home to a litany of jazz greats, from Buddy Bolden and Sidney Bechet, to Jelly Roll Morton and Louis Armstrong. Today Tremé remains one of the city's most vibrant African-American neighborhoods; unfortunately it's also plagued by crime, so don't walk there at night.

All That Jazz

It all began in Congo Square—now Louis Armstrong Park, a few blocks from the mansions of Esplanade Avenue—a central meeting place where slaves used to sing and dance in the first half of the 19C. Their African chants and rhythms eventually fused with West Indian musical traditions, and refined themselves in the bars and brothels of Storyville. What emerged was the only truly American music genre: jazz.

Uptown

Bounded by Louisiana Ave., S. Claiborne Ave., Leonidas St. & the Mississippi River.

A lively mecca of students and high society, the Uptown/university area is accessible by the **St. Charles Avenue Streetcar**★★ *(see Musts for Fun).* Some of the 25-room mansions have been divided into apartments, so it's not unusual for a group of hipsters to reside next door to one of the city's old-money families. Uptown is an umbrella term that encompasses the Garden District, the Lower Garden District, the Irish Channel and Riverbend, the neighborhood between Audubon Park and the bend of the Mississippi. It's here that you'll find Loyola and Tulane universities, as well as the urban oasis of Audubon Park and the zoo.

Audubon Park★★ – *6800 St. Charles Ave. See Parks and Gardens.*

Audubon Zoological Gardens★★ – *6500 Magazine St. See Musts for Kids.*

The Irish Channel

Bounded by Magazine Street and the Mississippi River, Louisiana Avenue, and the Central Business District, the Irish Channel is so named because of a mass immigration from Ireland during the 1800s. As was true in most big cities during the 19C, the Irish were considered lowly laborers, and used for the most dangerous of jobs, including digging the 6mi New Basin Canal, which was to link the Mississippi River to Lake Ponchartrain. Plagued by disease and weakened by back-breaking labor, thousands lost their lives digging the canal, which was used for a century before it was paved over. According to local lore, the Irish are responsible for the distinctive New Orleanian accent, which sounds more Brooklynese than Southern. A lively St. Patrick's Day Parade still takes place in the neighborhood each year, starting out from St. Alphonsus Roman Catholic Church on Constance Street *(between Josephine & St. Andrews Sts.),* where services used to be held in both Gaelic and English.

New Orleans has come a long way since the French established a settlement along the Mississippi River in 1718. Nevertheless, its past remains a vivid aspect of the Big Easy's present personality. Here are some historic highlights to put on your list.

Jackson Square★★

Bounded by Chartres, St. Philip, Decatur & St. Ann Sts.

You can usually hear Jackson Square before you see it. The historic green, which began as a military parade ground known as Place d'Armes in 1721, is now the colorful heart of the French Quarter. In 1851 the square was re-named Jackson Square to honor **Andrew Jackson** (1767–1845), hero of the battle of New Orleans and seventh president of the US. Jackson, who served two terms in Washington, led a ragtag group of volunteers to victory against the British in 1815. He is memorialized atop horseback in the center of the square, surrounded by the elegant **St. Louis Cathedral**★, government buildings and the c.1840 **Pontalba Buildings**★. Notice the inscription on the statue: "The Union must and shall be preserved," an ironic note dictated by Union soldiers who occupied the city during the Civil War.

Photo Ops

For a great view of Jackson Square, cross Decatur Street to **Washington Artillery Park**, a sidewalk amphitheater where still more street entertainers congregate. The park is situated atop a seawall, designed to keep the Mississippi River from flooding the city streets. Climb to the top of the steps for a bird's-eye **view**★★ of the entire square.

A meeting place for musicians, fortune tellers, street performers, artists and tourists, Jackson Square is also a vibrant outdoor market where vendors sell their wares. Horse-drawn carriages line up along the Square, offering rides and colorful city commentary *(see Musts for Fun)*.

Cabildo★★ – *701 Chartres St. See Museums.*

Presbytere★★ – *751 Chartres St., Jackson Square. See Museums.*

Beauregard-Keyes House & Garden ★

1113 Chartres St. 504-523-7257. Visit by guided tour only year-round Mon–Sat 10am–3pm. Closed major holidays. $5.

Well-to-do auctioneer Joseph Le Carpentier built this romantic Greek Revival house in the heart of the French Quarter in 1826. Le Carpentier included a side garden on the corner of Chartres and Ursulines streets—an unusual feature, as most French Quarter gardens were tucked away in walled courtyards. In 1833 the property came into the possession of John A. Merle, Switzerland's consul in New Orleans, and his wife, Anais Philippon Merle, who adopted the garden. Madame Merle planned and planted a formal French parterre garden here, enclosing it with brick walls outfitted with grille windows, to give passersby a glimpse of the greenery within.

The house takes its name from two of its later owners, however: Confederate general **Pierre G.T. Beauregard**—the commander who ordered the first cannon shot at Fort Sumter—who lived here briefly after the Civil War, and American author **Frances Parkinson Keyes**, who restored both the house and garden in the 1940s.

Frances Parkinson Keyes

Born in Charlottesville, Virginia where her father headed the Greek department at the University of Virginia, Frances Parkinson Keyes (1885–1970) published her first novel, *Old Grey Homestead* in 1919. Her husband, Senator Henry Wilder Keyes, died in 1938, after which time Francis began spending winters in New Orleans. There she devoted herself to writing and to restoring the French Quarter house she purchased in 1944.

Ignoring curious fans, who came daily to peer through her windows, Keyes eventually set up her study in the home's former slave quarters. She wrote more than 20 of her 51 books at the house, including *Dinner At Antoine's*, *Chess Player (Paul Morphy)*, and *Blue Camellia*. Today you can see Keyes' doll and costume collection here as well as Beauregard family heirlooms and portraits.

Gallier House ★

1132 Royal St. 504-525-5661. www.gnofn.org/~hggh. Open by guided tour only year-round Mon–Sat 10am–3:30pm. Closed major holidays. $6. Combination tickets available for Gallier House & Hermann-Grima House.

Noted New Orleans architect James Gallier, Jr., whose architect father designed **Gallier Hall** ★ *(see Landmarks)*, built this side-hall, Italianate townhouse as his own residence in 1857. Gallier the younger and his father also designed the Pontalba buildings, the old French Opera House (which burned in 1919) and the original St. Charles hotel.

The Gallier House has been lovingly restored and is grandly furnished in the style of an upper-middle-class family in the 1860s. Notable for its wrought-iron arches on the second-floor galleries outside, and inside for its Corinthian columns, etched-glass skylight and gas chandeliers, the house is open to visitors by guided tour. Docents lead groups through the interior garden, the elegant carriageway and the restored slave quarters. Take a moment to look through the carriageway; it may be the only one in the city with a carriage parked in it. Anne Rice fans should note that this was the house the author had in mind when she described Louis and Lestat's residence in *Interview with a Vampire*.

Lafitte's Blacksmith Shop ★

941 Bourbon St. 504-522-9377.

While certainly not as grand as the city's respectably restored historic homes, Lafitte's is one of the oldest Creole cottages in the city. Now a favorite watering hole for locals, Lafitte's was constructed c.1772, more than a decade before the 1788 fire that destroyed most of the city. Legend has it that the building was once home to the family of the infamous pirate, Jean Lafitte, who ran a legit blacksmith shop up front and sold his illegal booty to fencers out the back door. True or not, it makes for a good drinking story.

Longue Vue House & Gardens★

7 Bamboo Rd. 504-488-5488. www.longuevue.com. Visit by guided tour only year-round Mon–Sat 10am–4:30pm, Sun 1pm–5pm. Closed Easter Sunday, Thanksgiving Day & Dec 25. $10.

Often called the Versailles of New Orleans, this palatial Mid-City estate was created from 1939 to 1942 by the late philanthropists, Edgar Bloom Stern, a New Orleans businessman and cotton broker, and his wife Edith, daughter of Julius Rosenwald, CEO of Sears Roebuck. The Greek Revival-style mansion, designed for the Sterns by architects William and Geoffrey Platt, is surrounded by eight acres of lovely gardens. Renowned landscape architect Ellen Biddle Shipman is responsible for the gardens; she also gets credit for part of the interior design, which features fine American and English antiques, French and Oriental carpets, and a noteworthy collection of 18C English creamware.

What's Inside? – Three stories and 20 rooms filled with antiques and contemporary art include the Oriental-style dining room with its Chinese rice paper screens, and the drawing room, where the likes of Eleanor Roosevelt, Jack Benny, Pablo Casals and John F. Kennedy were entertained. The home's interior conveys a sense of a conservative upper-crust lifestyle from the 1930s and 40s, one that supported the likes of a Flower-Arranging Room and a Wrapping Room, used only to open mail and wrap presents.

Gardens – While Ellen Biddle Shipman was influenced by gardens in Europe, the eight-acres of plots she created for the Sterns has a more intimate feel than formal gardens abroad. From the **Wild Garden**, planted with wildflowers and Louisiana iris, to the magnificent **Spanish Court**, inspired by the 14C Generalife Gardens in Granada, Spain, the gardens are a delight in any season. You'll feel like you're worlds away from the city as you stroll the ambling forest paths, inhale the aroma of magnolias, camellias, roses, sweet olives, and oleanders, and listen to the lyrical sound of water splashing in fountains.

• **Discovery Garden** – This one will appeal to the kids. Here they can run through a bamboo tunnel, navigate an herb maze and dig for worms.

Pontalba Buildings★

[E] *refers to map in inside front cover. On St. Peter St. and St. Ann St., bordering Jackson Square. 504-568-6967.*

Credited by many historians as the first apartment buildings in the US, these redbrick Greek Revival row houses draped in filigreed wrought iron were completed in 1850 for the Baroness Micaela Almonester de Pontalba. The Baroness modeled the houses on her apartments in Paris, intending for them to be a haven for high French society at a time when unwelcome Americans settlers were establishing a presence in the Canal district nearby.

There are two sets of Pontalba Buildings: the first, a group of 16 town houses on St. Peter Street, is known collectively as the Upper Pontalba; the second group, the Lower Pontalba, faces St. Ann Street across Jackson Square. Baroness de Pontalba also erected the square's fantastic wrought-iron fencing and, in 1856, provided its trademark landscaping, planted in a sun pattern in honor of Louis XIV of France, the Sun King. Look for her initials, A and P, incorporated into the ironwork on the balconies.

1850 House

523 St. Ann St., in the Lower Pontalba Building. 504-568-6968. http://lsm.crt.state.la.us. Open year-round Tue–Sun 9am–5pm. Closed major holidays. $3 (buy tickets at the Presbytere, 751 Chartres St.).

This is the only apartment in the Pontalba Buildings that is open to the public. Restored in the style of a mid-19C middle-class Creole home, the 1850 House includes a kitchen furnished with antique utensils, a dining room with a table set for dinner and a nursery complete with antique dolls.

The other apartments in the building are occupied by 21C residents. Still as prestigious a place to live as it was when Baroness Pontalba resided here, the Pontalba Building's apartments have a years-long waiting list.

Buy a Gift, Take a Tour

The **1850 House Museum Store**, operated by the Friends of the Cabildo, has an impressive selection of French Quarter history books, and they offer guided walking tours of the French Quarter Historic District. Tours depart daily from the 1850 House *(Mon 1:30pm, Tue–Sun 10am & 1:30pm; no tours on state holidays; $10; call for information: 504-523-3939).*

St. Louis Cathedral★

725 Chartres St., Jackson Square. 504-525-9585. www.saintlouiscathedral.org. Open year-round Mon–Wed & Fri 9am–5pm, Thurs & Sat 9am–4pm, Sun 2pm–5pm.

What bride wouldn't want to get married in this fairy-tale castle of a church, with its grand three-steepled white facade? (If you're planning a wedding in New Orleans, be advised that the waiting list is long!) The official seat of the Archdiocese of New Orleans was established as a parish in 1720 and ranks as the oldest continuously operating cathedral in the US. Dedicated in 1851, the present structure is actually the third church on this site; a fire destroyed the first one, and the second version collapsed during a renovation in 1849. The cathedral as you see it now is built of wood covered with stucco, rather than stone like its European counterparts. Although the outside of the structure is grander than the inside, it's worth stepping in for a look or to take one of the free 15-minute tours offered several times a day.

The cathedral's 16ft-wide marble main aisle is the only thing left from the original structure. In the sanctuary, ten stained-glass windows depict the life of King Louis IX of France, who was canonized a saint by the Catholic Church. These windows are smaller than you'd expect to find in such a grand cathedral; they were made that way on purpose to better withstand the coast's hurricanes.

St. Anthony's Close – This small garden behind the cathedral contains a memorial to the victims of yellow fever, which plagued the mosquito-infested city in the 18C and 19C. Not always a holy place, legend has it that St. Anthony's Close was the city's dueling ground before it was sanctified by the church.

Pirates Alley

Notice the alleyway on the left leading to Royal Street between the cathedral and its flanking buildings. This is **Pirates Alley**, where Nobel Laureate author **William Faulkner** (1897–1962) lived on the ground floor of Number 624 and wrote his first novel, *Soldiers' Pay* in 1925. Faulkner would no doubt approve of the Faulkner House bookstore, which now occupies that space and specializes in rare and first editions—including those by Faulkner himself. Though privately owned, the house is open to tours by advance reservation *(504-586-1609)*.

Degas House

2306 Esplanade Ave. 504-821-5009. www.degashouse.com. Visit by guided tour only year-round Mon–Fri 9am–5pm, weekends 9am–3pm. $10.

The sole French Impressionist to have painted in America lived for a time in this 1852 Italianate building. **Edgar Degas** (1834–1917), whose mother was born in New Orleans, stayed here while visiting his French-Creole kin, the well-to-do Musson family. During his stay (October 1872 until March 1873), Degas is believed to have completed more than 20 paintings, including one of his sister-in-law Estelle Musson. *The Portrait of Estelle*, now hangs in the **New Orleans Museum of Art**★ *(see Museums)*, and his painting of *The Cotton Market* in New Orleans was the first piece he ever sold to a museum; it depicts his uncle, Michael Musson, who was active in the cotton business. You can see reproductions of these works on a tour of the house, which is now a B&B *(see Must Stay)*. In the 1920s the original dwelling was divided; one wing was moved several feet to the side to serve as a second residence. Degas' bedroom, which also served as his studio, was situated in the second building *(currently being restored)*. If you're a big fan of Impressionist art, you'll want to plan a stop here, since this is the only Degas residence open to the public anywhere. Just remember that you'll need an advance appointment to visit, unless you happen to be a guest at the inn.

Degas in New Orleans

In the wake of the 1871 Siege and Commune of Paris in which thousands were killed, Edgar Degas left Paris and came to New Orleans to visit his maternal relatives, the Mussons. Degas had roots in New Orleans: his mother was born here, and his great-grandmother once owned a home in the city *(see Pitot House)*. His younger brother, René, moved to New Orleans after he married Estelle Musson. (She and her descendants dropped the Degas name after René ran off with a neighbor's wife.) Degas spent nearly six months in New Orleans discovering "the customs of a people, that is to say their charm." Though the ravages of the Civil War were still evident in New Orleans, he found the postwar city attractive enough to inspire some of his finest paintings, most of which were portraits of family members.

Fairmont Hotel

123 Baronne St. 504-529-7111 or 800-527-4727. www.fairmont.com.

This local landmark, which began in 1893 as the Grunewald Hotel, has a long history of entertaining the rich and famous. Owner Louis Grunewald eventually sold the hotel and it was renamed for President Theodore Roosevelt. In its incarnation as the Roosevelt, the lodging became famous as the New Orleans home-away-from-home of Governor Huey Long, who was pals with the hotel's second owner, Seymour Weiss. Long spent so much time here that it was rumored he built a 90mi highway just so he'd have more direct access to the hotel from his office in the State capital of Baton Rouge.

Long was not the only politician drawn to the gracious halls of the hotel that became a Fairmont property in 1965. Eight US presidents have stayed under its roof, including Coolidge, Eisenhower, Kennedy, Ford, George H. Bush and Clinton. Celebrities flocked here as well, especially when the famed Blue Room knew its heyday from the early 1930s to the 70s. Marlene Dietrich, Jimmy Durante, Tony Bennett, Tina Turner and Frank Sinatra were just a few of the headliners who performed on the Blue Room stage.

Huey "Kingfish" Long

New Orleans has no shortage of colorful characters, and Huey Long definitely tops the list. Governor of Louisiana from 1928 to 1932, Long was elected to the US Senate in 1930 and was assassinated in 1935 at the age of 42. He hailed from one of the poorest towns in rural Louisiana, one of nine children born to hardscrabble farm stock. Lomg put himself through school, earned a law degree in record time and set his sights on being a power broker—a goal he exceeded during his brief lifetime.

Nicknamed "Kingfish" after a popular radio-show character, Long accomplished much good during his political tenure, yet his ends-justify-all-means philosophy created armies of enemies and inspired Robert Penn Warren's Pulitzer Prize-winning novel *All the King's Men*. At the end of his life, the governor's strong-arm tactics, graft and cronyism earned him the label "American fascist" in the *New York Times*. The forces behind his assassination are still a mystery, but subscribers to conspiracy theory are quick to point out that Long was killed a month after declaring his candidacy for the presidency of the United States.

Hermann-Grima House

820 St. Louis St. 504-525-5661. www.gnofn.org/~hggh. Visit by guided tour only year-round Mon–Fri 10am–3:30pm. Closed major holidays. $6. Combination tickets available for Hermann-Grima House and Gallier House.

This symmetrical, Federal-style brick mansion stands out dramatically from the rest of its French Quarter neighbors. Built in 1831 for German businessman Samuel Hermann, the house offers a peek into the lives of a wealthy Creole family living in antebellum New Orleans. The handsome mansion with its courtyard garden boasts the only horse stable and functional outdoor kitchen in the Quarter. Its American design, complete with a center hall and double-hung windows, was revolutionary at the time.

Several different families owned the house, which stretches from St. Louis Street to Conti Street, before it became a boardinghouse in the 1920s. Its historic restoration was meticulous, and knowledgeable docents make this one of the city's most historically accurate tours. At Halloween, the house is draped in black bunting and docents explain 19C mourning customs.

Old Ursuline Convent

1100 Chartres St. 504-529-3040. www.accesscom.net/ursuline. Visit by guided tour only year-round Tue–Fri 10am–3pm, weekends 11am–2pm. Closed Mon and major holidays. $5.

New Orleans' oldest surviving building somehow escaped the devastating fire that ravaged the city in 1788. This fine example of the French Colonial style was erected as a convent by architect Ignace Francois Broutin and builder Claude Joseph Villars Debreuil between 1745 and 1752, replacing an earlier compound built in the 1720s. Ursuline nuns first arrived from France in 1722, intent on their mission of healing the sick and teaching, both the children of the bourgeoisie and the less advantaged black and Indian population. Following the Natchez massacre, in 1729, the convent opened its doors to the orphaned children of the French colonists who were slaughtered at Fort Rosalie. You can still read the names of those who were killed . . . Louise Chalante, Francoise Caillon, Marie LePris, and so on . . . in the yellowing archives at the Convent.

St. Mary's Church – Adjacent to the convent, St. Mary's was built in 1845 as the chapel of the Archbishops. Today the pretty church, where Masses are still said daily, is also open for tours.

Pitot House Museum

1440 Moss St. 504-482-0312. www.pitothouse.org. Visit by guided tour only year-round Wed–Sat 10am–3pm. Closed major holidays. $5.

A graceful West Indies-style home, Pitot House is a rare example of a colonial dwelling remaining in New Orleans today. It was built in the 1790s on Bayou St. John and bears the name of one of its illustrious owners, James Pitot, a Haitian refugee who purchased it in 1810 from the great-grandmother of French painter Edgar Degas *(see Degas House)*.

The simple two-story country dwelling is now a museum, restored to its original appearance with stucco-covered brick and a hipped roof. Tours tell the story of life along Bayou St. John when the area was dotted with plantations. The house has been furnished with Louisiana and American antiques from the early 1800s in keeping with the style and period when James Pitot lived here. Notice the solid wood shutters, designed to close at a moment's notice in case of a hurricane. Purchased in 1904 for use as a convent by Mother Frances Xavier Cabrini, the first American to be canonized by the Catholic Church, the site was donated to the Louisiana Landmarks Society in 1962. The Society now uses the house as its headquarters and opens the home for tours.

Le Monde Creole Walking Tour★

624 Royal St. 504-568-1801. www.lemondecreole.com. Mon–Sat 10:30am & 1:30pm, Sun 10am & 1:30pm. $10. If you plan to visit **Laura Plantation★★** on River Road *(see Excursions)*, set the stage by taking Le Monde Creole walking tour of the French Quarter, based on the journal of Laura Locoul, a Creole woman and plantation mistress who lived in New Orleans in the 19C. You'll discover the European and African branches of this Creole dynasty and hear stories of Creoles, free people of color, and slaves. Offered in both French and English, the tour takes in hidden courtyards, the New Orleans Pharmacy Museum, the Hermann-Grima House, the Historic New Orleans Collection, and St. Louis Cemetery, where Laura's family is buried.

Parks and Gardens

From the canopies of live oaks that shade the Garden District to the lush courtyards and landscaped balconies of the French Quarter, the city's leafy pulse is easy to find. Flowers and plants grow so easily in New Orleans' sub-tropical climate that it's not unusual to see a feathery fern or a fragrant gardenia blossom straining its way through a crack in the concrete—beauty just has a way of finding the sun here.

Audubon Park★★

6800 St. Charles Ave., between Walnut St. & Exposition Blvd. 504-861-2537. www.auduboninstitute.org. The park is stop no. 36 (across from Tulane & Loyola universities) on the St. Charles streetcar.

Talent often runs in families: John Olmsted, son of Frederick Law Olmsted who designed Central Park in New York City, laid out Audubon Park in the late 19C. Shaded by giant live oaks and ancient magnolias, the 400-acre park offers miles of jogging, hiking, and biking trails, as well as a newly renovated **golf course** that stretches from the entrance at St. Charles Avenue to Magazine Street upriver behind the zoo. Dotting the area are lagoons filled with ducks, geese and swans, 10 public clay tennis courts, a public pool, bridle paths, ball fields and picnic tables. Take in an outdoor concert at Newman Bandstand— and don't forget the zoo, the park's biggest attraction.

Audubon Zoological Gardens★★ – *6500 Magazine St. See Must Sees for Kids.*

Cascade Stables – *700 East Dr., behind the zoo; 504-891-2246; open year-round Tue–Sun 8am–5pm.* Rent horses here for a trail ride around the park.

French Quarter Courtyards

There are so many reasons to love the Vieux Carré, but its flower-filled balconies and secret courtyard gardens are close to the top of the list. Although some are tended by shopkeepers and restaurants, most are lovingly landscaped by the Quarter's 3,000 or so residents, who often accent the plants with elaborate seasonal displays of lights for Christmas and festive purple, green and gold motifs for Mardi Gras. Beware of "rain" on a sunny day—most homeowners give their balcony plants a good dousing daily, and you're liable to get wet if you don't watch where you're going. Although most courtyards are tucked out of sight, many, like the one at the **Beauregard-Keyes House**★ *(See Historic Sites)* offer wrought-iron grills that give passersby the chance to peek inside.

City Park★★

1 Palm Dr. 504-482-4888. www.neworleanscitypark.com. Hours & fees vary for attractions.

City Park is to New Orleans what Central Park is to Manhattan. In fact, the 1,500-acre park is the fifth-largest swath of urban greenery in America, and twice the size of its New York counterpart. The land for City Park was drawn from the Allard Plantation, a gift to the city of New Orleans from philanthropist John McDonogh in 1854. Over the centuries, City Park's forest has grown to include some 14,000 mature trees divided among 50 species, including bald cypress, Southern magnolia, Southern pine, and the largest collection of mature live oaks in the world *(see sidebar below)*.

What's Doing in City Park?

Most of the park's attractions are concentrated in the lower part of the park, south of I-610.

Marconi Meadow – This 25-acre enclosed green space bounded by scenic lagoons, and groves of cypress, oak and magnolias, is used for festivals, open-air concerts and other events.

Peristyle – *At Dreyfous Ave.* Built in 1907, the Neoclassical dancing pavilion with its majestic columns makes an elegant place for a picnic. Nearby, the 1912 Casino now contains an ice cream parlor and snack bar.

Sports – Play, play, play. Here you'll find four golf courses; a public tennis center; 8mi of lagoons swimming with catfish, bass and perch; and 400-meter City Park Track, designed for the 1992 Olympics.

Why Are Those Trees Called "Live Oaks?"

Since you'll hear a lot about live oaks in New Orleans, here's the skinny. The live oak is unique among oak trees in that it is evergreen, or nearly so, since the old leaves drop at about the same time as the new leaves appear in the spring. Because it looks like the leaves never die, the trees were called "live" oaks. Characterized by its distinctive low-spreading form, a mature live oak can sprout lateral limbs that just about touch the ground, and branches that can extend out twice the height of the tree.

The oldest moss-draped live oaks in City Park line the vestiges of Bayou Metairie, an ancient tributary of the Mississippi River. The McDonogh, Dueling and Suicide oaks are estimated to be close to 600 years old, the remains of a forest that started long before Sieurs Iberville and Bienville first scouted the area for a settlement site.

More Fun in City Park

New Orleans Botanical Garden

Victory Ave., Mid-City 504-483-9383. www.citypark.com/garden. Open year-round Tue–Sun 10:30am–4:30pm. Closed Mon. $5.

Built by WPA workers during the Depression, the botanical garden opened as the City Park Rose Garden in 1936. After years of neglect, the seven-acre site was reborn in the 1980s as the New Orleans Botanical Garden, the result of a collaboration between New Orleans architect Richard Koch, landscape architect William Wiedorn, and artist Enrique Alferez. Noted for its striking collections of begonias, ferns and bromeliads, the garden contains some 2,000 varieties of plants set among the nation's largest stand of mature live oaks.

● **Conservatory** – The first phase of the renovation of the c.1930 Conservatory has restored it as a show place for plants. Future construction will add a desert environment, a mountain rain forest, and a French Quarter-style courtyard to display the garden's orchid collection.

● **Train Garden** – Newest feature of the Botanical Garden, the Train Garden reproduces the city's landmarks completely out of botanical materials. Miniature trains and streetcars ride along 1,300ft of track around this green "city" *(trains run Thu–Sun 10am–2pm, weather permitting).*

Longue Vue House and Gardens★ – *7 Bamboo Rd. See Historic Sites.*

New Orleans Museum of Art★ – *1 Collins Diboll Circle. See Museums.*

Carousel Gardens and Storyland – *Off Victory Ave. See Musts for Kids.*

Green Neutral Grounds

When you hear New Orleanians referring to "neutral grounds," they're talking about the medians that divide the city streets. Why do they call them that? It all goes back to the 1830s, when American settlers started arriving in town. Unwelcome by Creoles in the long-established French Quarter, the Americans settled upriver on the other side of Canal Street (the present-day Central Business District). Eventually, the median that divided Canal Street became the neutral ground between the two fractious groups.

There are "neutral grounds" all around the city; some are adorned with tropical foliage, civic monuments, playground equipment and sculptures. When it rains and the streets flood, cars take refuge there as well, since the neutral ground is ironically also the higher ground.

Woldenberg Riverfront Park

Along the Mississippi River from Canal to St. Louis Sts. 504-861-2537.

Thirteen acres of landscaped green space, stretching from the **Audubon Aquarium of the Americas**★★ *(see Musts for Kids)* to **Jax Brewery** *(see Must*

Shop), parallels the Mississippi River in the French Quarter, attracting joggers, in-line skaters and visitors in search of a waterfront view. Scattered throughout the park are shade trees, benches and sculptures, including Ida Kohlmeyer's whimsical *Aquatic Colonnade,* and John Scott's stainless-steel *Ocean Song (above).* At the uptown end of the park you'll find the Canal Street Ferry Landing.

New Orleans Jazz & Heritage Festival

Held at New Orleans Fair Grounds Race Course in late Apr–early May. 1751 Gentilly Blvd. 504-522-4786. www.nojazzfest.com. When the first New Orleans Jazz & Heritage Festival—better known as Jazz Fest—was held in Armstrong Park in 1969, the attendance was so sparse that students from a nearby school were invited to finish off the food. By 2004, its 35th anniversary, attendance has grown to between 75,000 and 100,000 music lovers a day.

The festival outgrew its Congo Square location long ago, relocating to the Fair Grounds for seven glorious days at the end of April. Now you can hear music at a dozen stages, from blues and jazz to rock and zydeco. Funky hats, decorated mambo sticks and all kinds of crazy outfits make for great people-watching among the mellow crowd. The musical line-up is a veritable who's who of local talent, along with national headliners like Paul Simon, Bob Dylan, Dave Matthews Band and Bonnie Raitt.

The event has become so popular that fans book accommodations and airfare months in advance. If you plan to attend, dress for comfort, and don't forget a hat and sunscreen (a rain poncho is a good idea, too). You can take a break from the sometimes sweltering heat at the oyster bar in the air-conditioned Race Course Clubhouse. Special concerts are scheduled around the city in the evenings, and with so much talent in town for the Fest, you never know who's going to show up for a jam session.

New Orleans is a city-wide museum, rich in art collections and historic homes reflecting its tumultuous past and Spanish, French, African and American heritage. From world-class art to quirky pocket museums housing important cultural treasures, New Orleans is ripe for discovering the past.

Historic New Orleans Collection★★

[D] *refers to map on inside front cover. 533 Royal St. 504-523-4662. www.hnoc.org. Open year-round Tue–Sat 10am–4:30pm. No admission for downstairs gallery; $4 for tour. Closed Jan 1, Mardi Gras day & Dec 25.*

This private archive is housed in a beautifully restored 18C Spanish Colonial manse that managed to survive the city's 1794 fire intact. Changing exhibits fill the ground-floor Williams Gallery, and an incredible group of maps, historic documents, drawings and sketches can be viewed on a guided tour of the 1792 Merieult House, which includes the **Louisiana History Galleries** upstairs. Compiling the Historic New Orleans Collection was the passionate project of the late General L. Kemper Williams and his wife, Leila, French Quarter preservationists who spent a lifetime chronicling their city's illustrious past. They purchased their residence, an 1889 Trapolin town house, in 1938 and lived there until 1964. After the general's death in 1971, the Williams' home was opened to the public.

The **research collection** is especially strong in documents relating to the Battle of New Orleans and the War of 1812 in the South, including rare books, maps and plans that collectively tell the story of one of the greatest military upsets of all time.

If time permits, take a tour of the **Williams' residence**, decked out with gorgeous early-20C Louisiana antiques and Chinese porcelains.

Boasting some 6,000 city-related documents, the **research center**, is staffed by helpful and knowledgeable history hounds, who can track down documents and materials relating to famous floods and fires, infamous town citizens like voodoo queen Marie Laveau, and architectural plans of some of the city's most famous buildings.

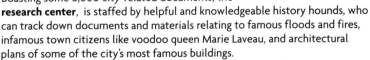

Shop at the Collection

Even if you're not a history buff, check out the collection's gift shop, accessible directly from Royal Street. Here you'll find an interesting array of antique jewelry, vintage prints and maps, antique silver, Victorian bric-a-brac, Mardi Gras memorabilia, porcelains, linens, vintage postcards, crystal and china, museum reproductions, and an extensive book department. And it's not all about capitalism—proceeds from all sales go to maintaining the Historic New Orleans Collection and the Williams Research Center.

Louisiana State Museums★★

French Quarter. The phone and Web site for all museum properties is the same: 504-568-6968 or 800-568-6968; http://lsm.crt.state.la.us. All sites are open year-round Tue–Sat 9am–5pm. Closed Mardi Gras day & major holidays. Combination tickets are available.

New Orleans' most prominent heritage attraction is the Louisiana State Museum, a complex of national land-marks housing thousands of artifacts and works of art reflecting Louisiana's legacy of historic events and cultural diversity. The museum operates five properties in the French Quarter: the Cabildo, Presbytere, 1850 House, Old U.S. Mint and Madame John's Legacy.

Cabildo★★

[A] *refers to map on inside front cover. 701 Chartres St. $5.*

Located in Jackson Square next to the St. Louis Cathedral, the Cabildo was built by the Spanish government between 1795 and 1799 to house offices of the town council. It is here that the history-making transfer papers for the Louisiana Purchase were signed in 1803. Today the Cabildo and the adjacent Arsenal contain a diverse collection of artifacts relating to Louisiana history. The museum prides itself on having one of the four original death masks made of French Emperor Napoleon in 1821.

Presbytere★★

[F] *refers to map on inside front cover. 751 Chartres St., Jackson Square. $5.*

Located to the right of St. Louis Cathedral, this c.1790 building—originally called the Ecclesiastical House—was constructed on the site of the 1720 residence, or presbytere, of the Capuchin monks. Be sure to go inside to see the permanent exhibit Mardi Gras: It's Carnival Time in Louisiana, where you can become a virtual krewe member *(see p 60)* and ride on a Mardi Gras float.

Madame John's Legacy

632 Dumaine St. $3.

This raised Creole cottage, one of the few 18C survivors in the Quarter, earned its enduring fame thanks to writer George Washington Cable, who used the house in his novella *Madame John's Legacy*, the story of how a quadroon, or mixed-race, mistress used her inheritance from her white lover. Separated by an L-shaped courtyard, the home's three buildings include a two-story *garçon-nière*, a stand-alone apartment that was used for older children or bachelors. Now the property of the Louisiana State Museums, the residence serves as a gallery and display space.

1850 House – *In the Pontalba Buildings, 523 St. Ann St. See Historic Sites.*

Old U.S. Mint – *400 Esplanade Ave. See p 55.*

Confederate Memorial Hall★

929 Camp St. 504-523-4522. www.confederatemuseum.com. Open year-round Mon–Sat 10am–pm. Closed Mardi Gras day and major holidays. $5.

Louisiana's oldest museum is home to the second-largest collection of Confederate memorabilia in the US, second only to the Museum of the Confederacy in Richmond, Virginia. Architect Thomas Sully designed this striking red stone Romanesque building, with its cypress woodwork and 24ft ceiling, in 1891.

Inside, more than 500 rare photographs offer a fascinating insight into early photography, with tintypes, ambrotypes, daguerreotypes, and *cartes de visites* portraying portraits of Confederate officers and soldiers. Personal memorabilia from President of the Confederacy, Jefferson Davis, is on exhibit, donated by his wife, Varina, when her husband died. His body laid in state at **Gallier Hall**★ *(see Historic Sites)* for two days, with some 60,000 people lining up to pay their respects. A collection of antique guns, swords and artillery completes the exhibits.

Battle Flags – More than 125 original battle flags of the South and the State of Louisiana are on display here, including the flag of Dreux's Battalion, commanded by Colonel Charles Dreux, the first Louisianan killed in battle; and a rather gruesome artifact, the Wheat's Battalion flag, stained with the blood of its commander, Roberdeau Wheat.

Tales of War

New Orleans was one of the first Southern cities to be occupied by Union troops, who marched into town in 1862 and stayed until the end of the war. The city didn't take kindly to its new regime or its new leader, General Benjamin F. Butler, who became infamous for ordering a man to be publicly hung on Esplanade Avenue for desecrating the Union flag. The women of the city reacted to this event with a showing of New Orleans sass—they vowed to ignore any Union soldier that crossed their path. The act of rebellion spurred Butler to display yet another show of dubious leadership, and decree that any woman who disrespected a Federal soldier would be jailed as a prostitute. You can see an entire case devoted to Butler on display at the Confederate Museum.

Musée Conti Wax Museum★

917 Conti St. 504-525-2605 or 800-233-5405. www.get-waxed.com. $6.75
Mon–Sat 10am–5pm, Sun noon–5:30pm Closed Dec 20–26 & Mardi Gras day.

More than 300 years of New Orleans history comes to life in tableaux featuring 154 lifelike wax figures including pirate Jean Lafitte, President Andrew Jackson, jazz great Louis Armstrong, voodoo queen Maria Laveau, and Mardi Gras Indian chief Montana. A "haunted dungeon" includes a few mild frights and the likes of Dracula and the Wolf Man.

How Do They Do That?

At the museum, every measure is taken to make the replicas look lifelike. Wax, mixed with chemicals to harden it and dye to color it, looks amazingly like human skin. In case you were wondering, the hair on the figures is human, inserted strand by strand; the heads are made in Paris; and the eyes are fashioned from special optical glass from Germany. Look closely at the male figures that don't have beards, and you'll see a slight stubble on their chins.

New Orleans School of Glassworks and Printmaking Studio★

727 Magazine St. 504-529-7277. www.neworleansglassworks.com. Open Sept–May Mon–Sat 10am–5pm. Rest of the year Mon–Fri 10am–5pm.

At this Warehouse Arts District studio, working artists demonstrate architectural glass blowing and other arts at the largest contemporary glassworking and printmaking facility in the South, a sister school of the Louvre Museum in Paris. Visitors are welcome to watch glass-blowing and casting techniques in front of an 850-pound recycling furnace filled with molten glass. A gallery and shop offers everything from art-glass goblets to specialty books and unusual glass architectural models for sale.

National D-Day Museum★

945 Magazine St. 504-527-6012. www.ddaymuseum.org. Open year-round daily 9am–5pm. Closed Jan 1, Mardi Gras day, Thanksgiving Day & Dec 25. $10.

Opened in 2000, this relative newcomer to the Warehouse Arts District is a moving tribute to the everyday heroes of World War II. The $21 million military archive was located in New Orleans because that was the home of Higgins Industries, the manufacturer of the landing craft that delivered US troops onto the D-Day beaches.

While this museum has both national and international scope, there are nonetheless many reminders of its ties to New Orleans, from an exhibit detailing the specifications of the Higgins boats—which were originally designed to travel on the bayou—to a replica of a Torpedo bomber plane flown by Louisiana veteran Commodore Thomas J. Lupo, which hangs in the Louisiana Memorial Pavilion. The museum recently launched plans to triple the size of its facility over the next five years.

Films – Start your visit at the Malcolm S. Forbes Theatre, where two films (shown alternately) will give you a sense of time and place, chronicling the compelling events in the Pacific Theater of World War II, from the bombing of Pearl Harbor in 1941 to the American occupation of Japan in 1945.

- *Price for Peace*, the evocative 45-minute film produced by Steven Spielberg and the late local historian Stephen E. Ambrose, includes interviews with war veterans (both American and Japanese) from all branches of the military.

- The documentary *D-Day Remembered* includes vintage clips of young American soldiers in training and in battle, as well as photographs from American, German and British archives.

Exhibits – Three floors of exhibits, 16,000sq ft in all, detail, in chronological order, Nazi aggression and propaganda, America's mobilization at home, the timeline of the Pacific Theater, and the sea and air assaults on the beaches of Normandy. Soldier's personal stories are relayed in mini theaters and oral-history booths throughout the galleries. But it's the personal mementos—a worn bible, hand-written letters home, a tattered uniform—that you'll remember most. If you're not up on your World War II history, consult the timeline wall and the huge interactive maps illustrating the geographical path of the war.

New Orleans Museum of Art ★

1 Collins Diboll Circle, in City Park. 504-488-2631. www.noma.org.
Open year-round Tue–Sun 10am–5pm. $6. Closed Mardi Gras day.

Head to lush City Park to take in this impressive collection of more than
40,000 works, including paintings, sculpture, photographs, decorative arts, and
more. European paintings here from France, Italy, Belgium and the Netherlands
span more than six centuries. American works range from 18C to present and
represent artists from John Singleton Copley to Georgia O'Keeffe. Native
American, pre-Columbian, Asian and African art rounds out the mix. New
Orleans Museum of Art's (NOMA) collection encompasses a survey of 19C and
20C Louisiana art.

NOMA also hosts blockbuster traveling exhibits. In 2003, *The Quest for Im-
mortality: Treasures of Ancient Egypt*, was the first ancient collection to tour
the US since the Tutankhamen and Ramses exhibitions in the early 1980s
(additional admission fees apply for big traveling exhibits).

Fabergé Treasures – On long-term loan to the museum, 57 masterworks by
Russian jeweler Peter Carl Fabergé include three of the renowned Imperial
Easter eggs and the impossibly delicate jewel-encrusted Lilies of the Valley
basket, made in 1896 and presented to the last Russian tsarina, Alexandra
Feodorovna, and considered by many to be Fabergé's greatest work.

French Connection – Reflecting the city's early heritage, the museum's collection of 19C and 20C French painting includes works by Impressionists Monet,
Gauguin and Degas, who spent time in New Orleans in the early 1870s.

Sydney and Walda Besthoff Sculpture Garden

The newly installed five-acre sculpture garden, which is free of charge, includes more
than 50 works by the likes of Henry Moore, Pierre Auguste Renoir and George Segal.
Museum docents lead guided tours through the rolling wooded setting daily at 11am
and 2pm. Native New Orleanians and city business and cultural leaders, Sydney and
Walda Besthoff are also avid art collectors. Sydney, who expanded his grandfather's
drug store business into six states, has been a longtime patron of the arts; New
Orleans' Contemporary Arts Center sits on the site of one of his old warehouses.

Ogden Museum of Southern Art, University of New Orleans★

925 Camp St. 504-539-9600. www.ogdenmuseum.org. Open year-round Tue–Sun 9:30am–5:30pm (Thu until 8:30pm). Closed Mon. $10.

The "O," as the Ogden Museum bills itself, is the place to gain an appreciation for Southern art—and the American South. A stunning 67,000sq ft complex affiliated with the Smithsonian Institution, the museum is home to one of the largest and most impressive assemblages of Southern art anywhere. The Ogden celebrates the South's vivid spirit and patchwork of cultures through its exhibits, but also through an ongoing program of lectures, films and music. Named for businessman and philanthropist Roger H. Ogden, who donated the 1,200 pieces that formed the core of the collection, the museum features works by artists in 15 states and the District of Columbia.

When you first walk into the Ogden's dramatic, four-story atrium with its floating staircase, you'll know you're in for a truly engaging experience. Before visiting the galleries, see the short film, narrated by Morgan Freeman, that introduces the Southern experience. Then wander through the museum's 20 galleries, where chronologically and thematically arranged exhibits chart major trends in the development of Southern art from the 18C to the 21C.

What's Up at the O?

- **Master of Glass** – This third-floor exhibit showcases the works of the North Carolina Penland School of Crafts. Spectacular pieces by Rick Beck, Gary Beecham, Stephen Dee Edwards, Robert Levin, Harvey Littleton, Mark Peiser and Richard Ritter are on display, part of a studio glass collection donated to the museum by Sonia and Isaac Luski of Charlotte, North Carolina.

- **Roger H. Ogden Collection** – Odgen's collection, recognized as the first to focus solely on Southern art, includes a significant group of works by Will Henry Stevens, one of the South's first Modernist painters.

- Take a break on the **rooftop terrace**, which offers a beautiful view of the city.

Contemporary Arts Center

900 Camp St at St. Joseph St. 504-523-1216. Box office: 504-528-3800. www.cacno.org. Galleries open year-round Tue–Sun 11am–5pm. Closed Mon. $5.

Dedicated to showcasing visual and performing artists, this industrial, light-filled former warehouse space includes more than 10,000sq ft of gallery space, two theaters with a lively schedule of productions by established and emerging playwrights, musical programming and even all-star jam sessions. Contemporary visual arts exhibits are always noteworthy; "Birdspace: A Post-Audubon Artists Aviary," in early 2004 looked at the prevalence of bird subjects in contemporary art since the early 1990s. The contrast between the work of John James Audubon, who was born outside of New Orleans, with work by local and national artists including Jacqueline Bishop, Ross Bleckner, Petah Coyne and Walton Ford, makes for striking imagery. CAC is well respected nationally, and its exhibits often travel around the country—Birdspace, for example, went to museums in Florida and Ohio.

> **Shhh...**
>
> Here's a secret that only the locals know: the museum's cafe includes two computers with free Internet access.

When you go in the lobby, be sure to notice the museum's front desk, created by sculptor Gene Koss as an undulating wave of glass plates.

What Else Do They Do?

As a multidisciplinary arts center with a mission to "support contemporary art, artists and emerging art forms," the CAC presents a year-round schedule of exhibits and performances to appeal to different sectors of the community. Everyone, from sophisticated art buffs to children, can find something to enjoy here. Past events have included jazz by Jane Monheit, an urban dance opera, sculptures by New Orleans artist Sally Heller, an exhibit of work by local public school students, and a monthly series of talks by Louisiana artists. There's even a gallery devoted to art for children, free for kids under age 15.

New Orleans Pharmacy Museum

[G] *refers to map on inside front cover. 514 Chartres St. 504-565-8027. www.pharmacymuseum.org. Open year-round Tue–Sun 10am–5pm. $5.*

Apothecary shop of the nation's first licensed pharmacist, Louis J. Dufilho Jr., this c.1823 building now houses a fascinating, and sometimes grim, collection of Civil War era-surgical tools, rare patent medications, live leeches and blood-letting instruments. There are plenty of "miracle" cures on hand, including the aphrodisiac Spanish Fly and Lydia Pinkham's famous vitamins that promised "a baby in every bottle," all displayed in gorgeous antique mahogany cabinets. Note the 1855 Italian marble soda fountain, guaranteed to make you pine for a malted. Donated to the collection by the St. Louis College of Pharmacy, the fountain pays homage to the tradition of soda fountains in drug stores, one that dates back to the 1830s, when pharmacists would mix phosphates and flavorings with bitter-tasting medicines to make them go down easier. The newly renovated walled courtyard is planted with traditional medicinal herbs.

How Do You Do That Voodoo?

Did you notice the gris-gris potions at the Pharmacy Museum? These were—and still are—used in the practice of voodoo. With its litany of spells, gris-gris, candles and charms, voodoo originated with Africa's Fon, Yoruba and Kongo tribes and has evolved into an exotic gumbo of traditional African spiritual beliefs blended with Catholicism. The practice of voodoo came to New Orleans with the slaves from West Africa and Haiti in the 1700s, and saw its zenith in the 1830s, during the reign of the celebrated mulatto priestess **Marie Laveau,** whose life is now the stuff of legend.

According to Priestess Miriam, who presides over the modern day **Voodoo Spiritual Temple** on the edge of the French Quarter in the Tremé neighborhood, voodoo is a religion long misunderstood. The modern practice of voodoo incorporates both white and black magic, with intense spirituality at its core.

To get in touch with your inner voodoo, visit the temple *(828 N. Rampart St.; 504-522-9627; www.voodoospiritualtemple.org)*, where blessings, African bone readings, rituals, potions and gris-gris are available. Or take one of the special voodoo tours, most of which include a visit to St. Louis Cemetery No. 1, where Marie Laveau is buried. The two-hour **Cemetery-Voodoo Tour** departs from the courtyard of Café Beignet *(334-B Royal St.; Mon–Sat 10am & 1pm, Sun 10am; $15; 504-947-2120; www.tourneworleans.com)*.

Old U.S. Mint

400 Esplanade Ave. 504-568-6968. http://lsm.crt.state.la.us. Open year-round Tue–Sat 9am–5pm. Closed Mardi Gras day & major holidays. $5.

Talk about a crisis of conscience—this National Historic Landmark has the interesting distinction of being the only place to mint coins for both the US and the Confederacy. Completed in 1835, the redbrick Greek Revival-style building was designed by prominent architect William Strickland, whose credits include the US Capitol in Washington, DC. The mint began operations in 1838, after President Andrew Jackson lobbied for its establishment to help finance development of the nation's western frontier. During the Civil War, the building was traded back and forth between the North and the South. After Louisiana seceded from the Union in 1861, the facility was used to house Rebel troops and to make coins for the Confederacy. When the Federal army occupied New Orleans the following year, the mint was put back to work for the federal government. It ceased operations once and for all in 1909, after turning out a sum total of about $300-million worth of gold and silver coins during its somewhat schizophrenic career. Once closed, the Mint was used for various official purposes, until it was transferred to the state and finally opened to the public as part of the Louisiana State Museums in 1981.

Jazz at the Mint

Run, don't walk, to this wonderful assemblage of jazz memorabilia on the second floor of the Old U.S. Mint. Here you'll see Louis Armstrong's cornet, Sidney Bechet's soprano sax and Dizzy Gillespie's trumpet with its famous "bent" bell. Relive the birth of jazz as it's chronicled in 10,000 photographs dating back to the 1950s at the New Orleans Jazz Club. Pictures of Jelly Roll Morton onstage, Duke Ellington at Jazzfest 1970 and Louis Armstrong as King Zulu at Mardi Gras in 1949 are priceless. Original recordings, from piano rolls to vinyl and digital tape include live performances, taped interviews and one-of-a-kind studio recordings.

New Orleans isn't known for its impressive skyline. But it does have its share of architectural and natural landmarks, the most noteworthy of which is the Mississippi River, the very reason French explorers founded the city here in the first place.

Gallier Hall ★

545 St. Charles Ave., Central Business District. Not open to the public.

You might find it odd that a building modeled on the Parthenon in Athens, Greece, symbolized all that was American in New Orleans, but that was, in fact, the case. At the time Gallier Hall was being constructed on Lafayette Square (1845–1853), the area west of Canal Street was the epicenter of the American population in New Orleans. This stately Greek Revival structure represented the fact that the Yankees were here to stay, much to the chagrin of their Gallic neighbors in the French Quarter just downriver.

Made of Tuckahoe marble and fronted by massive Ionic columns supporting figures of Justice, Liberty and Commerce, Gallier Hall served as the City Hall for more than a century, shifting the city's base of power from the Creole-dominated French Quarter to the American sector.

Over the years, various New Orleans' VIPs from Jefferson Davis and General P.G.T. Beauregard to local musical legend Ernie K-Doe (2001) have lain in state here. During Mardi Gras, the city's mayor traditionally watches the parades from the Gallier Hall steps, where he is toasted by the king or queen of each passing procession.

What's in a Name? – Credit for the design of Gallier Hall goes to Irish architect James Gallier, Sr. Ironically, before coming to New Orleans, Gallier changed his name from Gallagher to Gallier in hopes of being better accepted by the city's Creole society. Apparently it worked, since Gallier's later commissions included the 1858 French Opera House (which burned in the early 19C).

Lafayette Square

Bounded by St. Charles Ave. & Camp St., between Girod & Poydras Sts.

Named for the French hero of the Revolutionary War, the Marquis de Lafayette, this square facing Gallier Hall in today's Central Business District was the center of life for Americans living in New Orleans in the early 19C. The expanse of green, laid out in 1788, is the city's second oldest; only Jackson Square predates it. Among the statues that grace the square are images of Ben Franklin, statesman Henry Clay and local philanthropist John McDonough, whose belief that slaves should be educated led him to bankroll the city's free public schools.

First NBC Center

201 St. Charles Ave.

Built in 1974 by Moriyama & Teshima Architects of Toronto, this award-winning office tower stands at 645ft and rises to 53 stories. It's the second-highest building in New Orleans, with only One Shell Square overtopping it at 697ft. Also known as Place St. Charles, NBC Center occupies the former site of the St. Charles Hotel, once one of the city's most luxurious lodgings. In fact, the building's crown recalls the lantern atop the hotel, which served to guide ships up the river. At the center's base is a two-level galleria of shops and cafes.

Stella Jones Gallery

201 St. Charles Ave., on the ground floor of First NBC Center. 504-568-905. www.stellajones.com.

Stella Jones is the place to come for superior works of art by local and national artists of the African diaspora. The impressive roster of artists represented here includes Richmond Barthe, Elizabeth Catlett, Richard Hunt and Tunde Afolayan Famous, Jr. Exhibits change monthly from April through December. The gallery also offers lectures, exhibits with artists in attendance, and educational programs for African-American youth.

Louisiana Superdome

Sugar Bowl Dr. Box office: 504-587-3800. Tour information: 504-587-3808. www.superdome.com.

The city's largest and most famous sports venue is the Louisiana Superdome, considered cutting-edge in arena design when it was built in 1975. Home to the annual Nokia **Sugar Bowl,** the Superdome boasts the world's largest continuous roof without interior support.

Home field for the New Orleans Saints NFL football team, the Superdome can accommodate a wide range of events from a visit from Pope John Paul II to a Rolling Stones concert to traveling rodeos and monster truck pulls. Thanks to the Superdome, New Orleans has been able to play host to nine Super Bowl games (the most recent in 2002), several men's and women's basketball Final Four NCAA championships; and the College World Series in 2001.

Superdome Fast Facts

- The imposing steel dome is 27 stories high.

- It covers a 52-acre footprint.

- The Superdome holds 80,000 fans when it's filled to capacity.

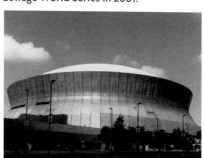

Mississippi River

New Orleans' most obvious landmark might be easy to overlook if you don't look beyond the glitz and feathers of the French Quarter. That landmark is the Mississippi River, which stretches 2,350mi from Lake Itasca in Minnesota to the Gulf of Mexico.

Defining the city's famous crescent outline, the Mississippi has also shaped New Orleans history. In the late 18C and early 19C, the waterway brought big wealth to the city in the form of river commerce. Today the port of New Orleans outstrips all other US ports in terms of total tonnage, averaging 11.2 million tons a year, and leading the nation in the import of natural rubber, coffee and steel. Over the years, however, the Father of Waters has not always been kind; disastrous floods have destroyed many lives and much property in low-lying New Orleans.

New Orleans from the Water – For a peek at the city from a different perspective, wander down to the riverfront and hop aboard a paddlewheeler *(see Musts for Fun)*. Watch the constant boat traffic and listen to the churning engines that make up the river's soundtrack. Mark Twain once said that the Mississippi river is a wonderful book with a new story to tell every day. If you listen hard enough, maybe you'll hear it, too.

A Sense of Direction

Ask a native New Orleanian which way is up and he may just scratch his head. The locals' skewed sense of place is based on the river's crescent curve that turns everything upside down, creating a maze of loopy streets in a city nearly surrounded by water.

Ask somebody to pinpoint a building's location, and you might hear "it's on the downtown, lakeside corner." And if that isn't confusing enough, if you're on the east bank of the river downtown and you need to head to the west bank, you go east. In fact, if you're going to understand New Orleans geography at all, your best bet is to give up your compass altogether. Locals don't give directions in terms of east, west, north and south. Instead, they'll point you:

- Uptown – Upriver toward the Garden District and beyond.
- Downtown – Beginning in the Central Business District and extending through the French Quarter.
- Lakebound – Toward Lake Pontchartrain on the city's northern border.
- Riverbound – Refers, of course, to the Mississippi.

U.S. Custom House

423 Canal St.

Home to the city's maze of customs offices, this imposing Greek Revival structure takes up the entire block of Canal Street between North Peters and Decatur Street in the French Quarter. It's made of marble quarried in Massachusetts, and each side of the building is lined with rows of fluted columns topped by Egyptian capitals.

When work began on the Custom House in 1848, it had the dubious distinction of being the most expensive federal project ever designed—and ended up taking 33 years to complete. Conflicts with the building's series of architects and the intervention of the Civil War slowed progress on the Custom House, which wasn't finished until 1881.

Great Marble Hall – Step inside to see the impressive light-filled space that rises 54ft to a skylight sitting on 14 massive Corinthian columns.

> **Fun Fact**
>
> Fate's a funny thing. In 1853 US Army captain P.G.T. Beauregard was appointed Superintendent of Construction for the U.S. Custom House. Beauregard, of course, would later rise to fame as a general in the Confederate army.

World Trade Center

2 Canal St., at the river. 504-529-1601. www.wtc-no.org.

Inside the World Trade Center's ground floor you'll find a colorful collection of flags, evidence of the many consulates and foreign agencies housed here. Built in 1965, the 407ft-tall office tower overlooks the Mississippi River; it was the first member of the World Trade Center organization that now includes more than 300 sites.

Go For a Spin – Take a trip up to the 33rd floor of the World Trade Center, where the revolving cocktail lounge, called **360,** provides the best cityscape and river **view★★★** in town. The deck travels at a leisurely 3ft per minute, making one complete revolution every hour and a half. Stop by for a cocktail and catch the sunset—there isn't a bad seat in the house *(504-522-9795).*

Spanish Plaza – *Facing the World Trade Center along the riverfront, between Canal & Poydras Sts.* Located below the World Trade Center and providing an entrance into **Riverwalk Marketplace** *(see Must Shop),* this expansive tile plaza with its large fountain was a gift from Spain for the nation's bicentennial. Special events and concerts are held here year-round, including a raucous masked ball on the eve of Mardi Gras, which is open to the public free of charge.

Musts for Fun

Fun and the Big Easy go together like café au lait and beignets, sequins and Mardi Gras, crawfish and étoufée. You get the idea . . . your only problem will be making time for all the fun you want to have while you're in town.

Biggest Party in Town: Mardi Gras★★★

World renowned as an unabashed invitation to escapism and decadence, Mardi Gras is the final hurrah before the spartan period of Lent. The Carnival season officially kicks off on Twelfth Night, January 6, with dozens of parades, balls and parties leading up to **Fat Tuesday** (*Mardi Gras* in French) the day before Lent, when the entire city closes up and lets its hair down.

Historically, Mardi Gras dates back to the 1740s, when the city's French governor instituted regular masked balls, much to the delight of the majority of the population. A movement by some of the city's more sober citizens to ban all public carnival celebrations was thwarted by a group of hard-core revelers who formed the first Mardi Gras organization—or krewe—to keep the parties going. Today every krewe has its own king and queen, but Rex, the King of Carnival, and his queen are the undisputed rulers of Mardi Gras.

While the balls are mostly private affairs, the parades are public spectacles. Each year, diehard revelers don the colors of Mardi Gras—green, purple and gold—and pack themselves like sardines into the streets to vie for the strings of plastic beads and other trinkets that riders aboard the floats toss into the crowd. It's not uncommon to see the more nubile young partyers bare their breasts to earn a handful of cheap plastic beads. After all, anything can happen once the King of Rex has officially banished "the commonplace of daily existence" from the city.

How Do I Get To Mardi Gras?

The answer to this commonly asked tourist inquiry is: You don't. Mardi Gras is not a place. There is no one celebration, instead there are myriad parades in every neighborhood in town—although not on Bourbon Street, because of the massive crowds. If you don't want to fight the crowds along the parade routes, many restaurants will rent you a place on their balcony. *For details about Mardi Gras, contact the New Orleans Convention and Visitors Bureau (800-672-6124; www.nawlins.com).*

Ride the St. Charles Avenue Streetcar★★

For schedules, call the NORTA Rideline: 504-827-7802. www.regionaltransit.org.
$1.25 (exact change required).

Built for commuters in 1831, the
St. Charles Avenue Streetcar is
still the only public transport
along St. Charles Avenue. This
National Historic Landmark,
which runs for 13mi from Canal
Street along St. Charles to Carrollton Avenue, is a great way to
take in the sights of the Garden
District, and travel uptown to
the Audubon Zoo, Tulane Univer-
sity, Carrollton and Riverbend—a 45-minute trip one way if you don't stop. Part of
the NORTA (New Orleans Regional Transit Authority) system, the streetcar line is
the oldest in the country; the original cars were pulled by mules. Even the
"modern" olive-green electric cars date back to the early 1900s. If you want to
see the sights, avoid the streetcar during rush hours *(7am–9am & 4pm–6pm)*.

Steamboatin' on the Mississippi★

Seeing New Orleans from the Mighty Mississippi offers a whole new perspective on the city—one shared by the likes of Mark Twain and other famous
passengers over the years. Fees and schedules vary, depending on the type of
cruise; call or check online for details.

Steamboat Natchez – *Departs daily from*
the Toulouse St. Wharf, across from Jackson
Square. 504-586-8777 or 800-233-2628.
www.steamboatnatchez.com. Patterned
after the 19C Ohio River sternwheeler
packets, the modern-day version
(launched in 1975) can accommodate
1,600 passengers for lunch and dinner
cruises in air-conditioned comfort—

something that was unheard of in packetboat days. Listen for the sound of the
Natchez's steam calliope when you're walking along the riverfront.

Cajun Queen and Creole Queen – *Depart year-round from the dock at the*
Aquarium of the Americas (end of Poydras St.). 504-524-0814 or 888-311-4109.
www.neworleanspaddlewheels.com. Options for rides on these two paddle-
wheelers include a one-hour harbor cruise and a trip to historic Chalmette
Battlefield *(see Excursions)*.

John James Audubon – *Canal Street Dock at the Aquarium of the Americas.*
504-586-8777 or 800-233-2628. www.aquariumzoocruise.com. The *Audubon*
takes passengers on a 7mi journey between the Audubon Zoo and the
Aquarium of the Americas *(see Musts for Kids)*.

Take a Swamp Tour

Less than an hour outside of New Orleans you'll find a moss-draped world of bayous and swamps, populated by alligators, otters, turtles and all manner of water birds. Skimming along the bayou is a mighty nice way to recharge your batteries when they get worn down by the excess of the city.

Most tours last about two hours and include transportation from your hotel (rates quoted include transportation—it's less expensive from the dock).

Lil' Cajun Swamp Tours – *Hwy. 301, Crown Point. 504-689-3213 or 800-25-3213. www.lilcajunswamptours.com. $31.* These excursions use large boats, seating up to 67 people.

Dr. Wagner's Honey Island Swamp Tours – *Tours depart from Crawford Landing, on the West Pearl River in Slidell. Reservations required: 985-641-1769. www.honeyislandswamp.com/drpaul.html. $45.* Wetlands ecologist Paul Wagner leads informative tours of Honey Island's protected cypress swamp.

Cypress Swamp Tours – *On Bayou Segnette. 504-581-4501 or 888-554-8574. www.cypressswamp.com. $39.* This one takes you through Bayou Segnette.

Jean Lafitte Swamp Tour – *Off Hwy. 3134 in Marrero. 504-587-1719 or 800-445-4109. www.jeanlafitteswamptour.com. $42.* Slide through the waterways of Bayou Barataria with a native Cajun guide.

Tour the Cities of the Dead

Thanks to the city's notoriously high water table, coffins have an unsettling habit of refusing to stay buried—hence the necessary practice of entombing the deceased aboveground. Called "cities of the dead," New Orleans' pictur-esque cemeteries come complete with avenues lined with graves designed like miniature temples. It's dangerous to visit these sites alone, so plan to take a guided group tour.

Each cemetery has its own personality: Metairie Cemetery is known for its gaudy tombs; St. Louis No. 1 is distinguished by its unusual dark tombs; and Lafayette Cemetery claims some of the city's earliest settlers.

• **Save our Cemeteries** *(504-525-3377 or 888-721-7493. www.saveourcemeteries. org)* offers reliably good tours.

Breakfast at Café du Monde

800 Decatur St. 504-525-4544. www.cafedumonde.com.

No visit to New Orleans is complete without a stop at this French Quarter cafe for beignets—square fried doughnuts without the hole, doused in powdered sugar—and café au lait. A tradition here since the 1860s, Café du Monde is open 24 hours a day, seven days a week, and closes only, as the menu notes, for "Christmas and some hurricanes."

French Quarter Carriage Ride

Decatur St. at Jackson Square, French Quarter.

Mule-drawn carriage tours of the French Quarter are a popular tourist attraction, much loved for their open-air views and notoriously colorful—though not always historically accurate—city commentary. Prices for a 20- to 30-minute ride varies ($10/person is the average fare). Unlike a taxi stand, you aren't required to take the first mule in line, so walk up and down the queue until a mule-carriage-driver combo strikes your fancy.

Sip a Sazerac Cocktail at the Sazerac Bar

At the Fairmont Hotel, 123 Baronne St. 504-529-711. www.fairmont.com.

Whether, as locals claim, the Sazerac was indeed the first cocktail ever made remains a matter of debate. What is known is that the intimate Sazerac Bar in the Fairmont Hotel is the best place to sip one of these drinks, invented in the 1830s by apothecary Antoine Amadie Peychaud, creator of Peychaud Bitters. Peychaud's original recipe called for cognac, bitters, absinthe, sugar and water. That drink later became known as the Sazerac cocktail (so-named for a particular label of brandy). Absinthe was banned in 1912, replaced in the mix by other anise-flavored liqueurs like Pernod, Herbsaint or Ricard. There have been several Sazerac bars over the years, but the most popular one moved in 1949 to the Roosevelt Hotel, now the Fairmont.

A tip for the uninitiated: if you order a Sazerac rocks, the bartender will know you're a rookie—traditionally this drink is served neat.

Why Is It Called A Cocktail?

In the 1830s after Antoine Peychaud opened his Pharmacie Peychaud on Royal Street, he became locally famous for a drink he made for his friends. He served the toddy in a *coquetier* (French for "egg cup"). Local lore has it that the mispronunciation of coquetier eventually became the word cocktail—now forever enshrined in our libation lexicon.

It's no coincidence that Louisiana license plates feature the slogan "Sportsman's Paradise." Anglers, hunters, nature lovers and water-sports enthusiasts have myriad choices for outdoor recreation in the New Orleans area, much of it within easy driving distance of town. A word of warning: If you're going to be spending time in the bayous and swamplands, don't forget your insect repellant.

Barataria Preserve★

Barataria Visitor Center located 17mi south of New Orleans near Crown Point. 6588 Barataria Blvd. (Hwy. 45). 504-589-2330. www.nps.gov/jela. Park open Apr–Oct daily 7am–7pm. Rest of the year daily 7am–5pm.

A hideout for pirate Jean Lafitte and his cronies in the early 1800s, this segment of the Jean Lafitte National Historical Park and Preserve now protects

20,000 acres of hardwood forest, cypress swamp and freshwater marsh. Take a free ranger-led walk or a canoe trip through Barataria's 20mi of waterways. Feeling intrepid? Strike out on your own along one of the nine trails (most paved or on elevated boardwalks), that weave through the wetlands; keep your eyes out for migratory birds and wild iris in the spring. The on-site visitor center *(open year-round daily 9am–5pm; closed Mardi Gras day & Dec 25)* provides maps and information along with educational exhibits about the park's ecosystems, and a look at the swampland inhabitants over the centuries. If you're short on time, the 1.8mi **Coquille Trail** will give you a good introduction to the wetlands.

Stop by the park's French Quarter visitor center *(419 Decatur St.; 504-589-2133; same hours as Barataria visitor center)* for a full schedule of park activities and ranger-guided hikes and canoe trips *(reservations required)*.

Sighting the Purple Martin

Even the birds come in Mardi Gras colors in New Orleans. Purple martins, the largest member of the swallow family, are recognizable by their deep purple hue and beautiful song. These migratory birds begin to arrive in New Orleans in late January; they gather here en masse through the spring and are gone by November. New Orleanians prize martins for their voracious appetite—a hungry martin can eat up to 2,000 mosquitoes a day, a real blessing in these buggy parts.

If you want to see martins near the city, head upriver along the path that follows the levee on the south shore of Lake Ponchartrain. In spring and summer, thousands of purple martins roost in the understructure of the Causeway Bridge; watch for them at dusk as they leave their nests.

Bayou Sauvage National Wildlife Refuge

61389 Hwy. 434, Lacombe. 15mi east of New Orleans via I-10 East, I-510 & Hwy. 90 east. 985-882-2000. http://southeastlouisiana.fws.gov/bayousauvage.html.

Nesting pelicans, bald eagles, wading birds, alligators, swamp rabbits and nutria are just a few of the species of animals that inhabit the freshwater and brackish marshes, bottomland hardwood forests, lagoons, canals, chenieres (former beach fronts), and natural bayous of the country's largest urban wildlife refuge. Managed by the U.S. Fish and Wildlife Service, Bayou Sauvage claims a great **bike trail.** The paved, level 10mi loop along Lake Ponchartrain's shore here will take you through marshland where, if you're lucky, you might spot bald eagles or other endangered species.

Lake Pontchartrain

5mi north of the French Quarter via Elysian Fields Ave.

Part of an impressive estuarine system that drains into the Gulf of Mexico, Lake Pontchartrain claims a surface area of 629sq mi. The lake was named in 1699 for Count de Pontchartrain, who served as the minister of finance under Louisiana's namesake, King Louis XIV. Long a source of recreation for New Orleanians, who boat, fish and windsurf in its waters, Lake Pontchartrain stretches 40mi in length. Its 24mi width is spanned by the **Pontchartrain Causeway,** the world's largest over-water bridge.

In the early 20C, the lake played a role in the development of jazz—juke joints, fish camps and roadhouses sprang up around its shores during prohibition, with musicians like Buddy Bolden and Louis Armstrong on hand to entertain the rowdy crowds.

Lakeshore Park – Picnic areas and playgrounds abound along the 10mi strip of green that borders the south shore of Lake Pontchartrain. The park is a great place to walk, bike, in-line skate or simply kick back and watch the sunset.

Gone Fishin'

Southeast Louisiana's inland bays, lakes, bayous and wetlands offer ample opportunities for fishing in both fresh- and saltwater. Lake Pontchartrain itself is home to some 125 species of fish, including red snapper, speckled trout, largemouth bass and trigger fish. For information on fishing licenses, call the Louisiana Department of Wildlife & Fisheries *(888-765-2602; www.wildlifelicense.com).*

To arrange a fishing trip in the area, try one of the following outfits:
- **Bunch's Fishing Charters** – *Marrero, LA. 504-340-1510. www.flyfishingneworleans.com.*
- **Adventure South Guide Service** – *Buras, LA. 504-392-1700. www.adventure-south.com.*
- **Joe's Landing Marina** – *Barataria, LA. 504-689-7966. www.joeslanding.com.*

Despite its reputation as a city for grown ups who love to eat, drink, party and stay up late, New Orleans offers plenty of diversions for little ones in and around town. If you want the kids to tolerate your trips to the art museums, promise them an afternoon at the aquarium or the zoo.

Audubon Institute Attractions

The Institute is an umbrella organization that incorporates attractions located all over town, from the aquarium to the zoo to the nature center and the soon-to-open **Insectarium** (scheduled for fall 2004). The Institute, park and zoo were named for the famous ornithologist and painter **John James Audubon** (1785–1851), who spent many years working in and around New Orleans.

Audubon Aquarium of the Americas★★

Foot of Canal St. at the riverfront. 504-581-4629 or 800-774-7394. www.auduboninstitute.org/aoa. Open year-round Sun–Thu 9:30am–6 pm, Fri & Sat 9:30am–7pm. $15 adults, $8 children (2-12). Combination tickets including IMAX & zoo are available ($19–$27 adults, $11–$15 children).

Get up close and personal with some 10,000 finny creatures, including sharks, penguins sting rays and sea turtles at this colorful family attraction, located, fittingly, right on the river. The aquarium is designed to take you on a journey through the major aquatic habitats of North and South America, as well as introducing you to the denizens of local waters in the **Mississippi River Gallery.**

Try to catch at least one of the daily penguin and shark feedings; schedules are posted at the entrance.

Fish Stories

Gulf of Mexico – The Aquarium's diverse shark collection is contained in the 400,000-gallon Gulf of Mexico tank. Besides menacing 10ft-long sharks, you'll also see endangered sea turtles, stingrays and the largest tarpon in captivity. A touch pool nearby invites kids of all ages to pet a baby shark and handle other cool sea animals.

Seahorse Gallery – Besides tiny seahorses, this gallery's graceful inhabitants include gossamer seadragons. With flowing appendages that look like wings, these whimsical creatures resemble mystical sea monsters. Native to Australia, they're members of the same family of bony fishes as seahorses, but look more like floating foliage than spiny little dragons.

Caribbean Reef – Take a walk through a 30ft-long aquatic tunnel, where you'll be surrounded by 132,000 gallons of water. Everywhere you look, you'll see hundreds of colorful fishy reef residents gliding by. Every day at 4:30pm you can watch divers interact with the reef's fish.

Those Crazy Otters – Be sure to spend some time with Buck and Emma, two resident sea otters who live on the second floor. You can watch the otters' antics through large acrylic windows as they frolic in two pools and a waterfall. A big proponent of conservation, the aquarium cooperates with Monterey Bay Aquarium in California in its rehabilitation project for Southern sea otters. The program both rehabilitates otters and returns them to the ocean, or, as is the case with Buck and Emma, works to protect the species by breeding them in captivity (it hasn't happened yet, but Buck and Emma are working on it).

Coming Attractions: Audubon Insectarium

US Custom House, 423 Canal St., French Quarter. www.auduboninstitute.org/insect.

Been yearning to see the world's largest cockroach? Well, you'll be able to do it in the Audubon Institute's new Insectarium. Slated to open in late fall 2004, this $15 million facility will be located in the French Quarter's historic **U.S. Custom House** *(see Landmarks)*. The Insectarium will harbor the largest bug collection in the country, introducing some of the world's 1,000,000 known species of insects—poor misunderstood critters that they are. Several rooms will be devoted to the ornery species that plague New Orleanians, including termites, cockroaches and mosquitoes.

If you're hungry, be sure to catch a Cooking Show, where bugs—a great source of protein!—will be on the menu. Or walk through Butterflies in Flight, a Japanese-inspired garden populated by hundreds of free-flying butterflies. At the Field Camp you'll meet some creepy-crawlies face to face.

Audubon Zoological Gardens★★

6500 Magazine St. 504-581-4629 or 800-774-7394. www.auduboninstitute.org/zoo. Open late Mar–Oct 9:30am–5pm, weekends 9:30am–6pm. Rest of the year daily 9:30am–5pm. Closed Mardi Gras day, first Fri in May, Thanksgiving Day & Dec 25. $11 adults, $6 children (ages 2–12).

They say it's all happening at the zoo—and they're right. With innovative natural habitats housing some 1,500 exotic animals from rare white alligators to majestic Bengal tigers, it's no wonder the 53-acre Audubon Zoo is one of the area's favorite family gathering spots.

What's What at the Zoo

Asian Domain – This is where you'll find two of the zoo's most popular residents: Rex and Zulu, the rambunctious white tiger brothers. The Indian tigers live in this lush landscape along with Malayan sunbears and Asian lions.

Louisiana Swamp – Don't have time for a swamp tour? You can get a slice of bayou life at the zoo. Come tour this Cajun village, complete with cypress knees, Spanish moss and gators galore.

Just for Kids –A highlight at the new **Children's Zoo** is the endangered-animal carousel. Hop on one of 60 different figures—from traditional horses to elephants, rhinos, giraffes and other vanishing species ($2). Rolling down **Monkey Hill**—billed as the tallest point in New Orleans—has been one of the highlights of a visit to Audubon Zoo for generations. Now a new three-tiered treehouse here gives visitors a "monkey's-eye view" from atop its 20ft-high platform.

Get Interactive – Watch lovable sea lions show off; catch a performance of Zieux Orleans (musicals with animal stars); take a Discovery Walk; or visit the Embraceable Zoo, where you can have a close encounter with endangered domestic animals.

All in a Day's Fun

Why not make a day of it? For a real treat—one the kids will love—buy a combination ticket for the zoo and the aquarium, and take the *John James Audubon* riverboat to cruise from place to place *(504-586-8777; see Musts for Fun)*. It sure beats driving.

Audubon Louisiana Nature Center

5601 Read Blvd., in Joe W. Brown Memorial Park. Take I-10 East to Read Blvd. exit and continue south to park. 504-246-5672 or 800-774-7394. www.auduboninstitute.org/lnc. Open year-round Tue–Fri 9am–5pm, Sat 10am–5pm, Sun noon–5pm. Closed Mon. $5 adults, $3 children (ages 2–12).

This eco treasure east of town offers an outstanding array of science and nature activities, including a planetarium, a butterfly garden, a bee aviary and a turtle pond. Elevated boardwalks and trails lead you through the swamps of an 86-acre bottomland hardwood forest, where you're likely to see all kinds of Louisiana critters, from tortoises and great blue herons to alligators.

The newest permanent exhibit, **Louisiana Habitats and Habits,** deals with the remarkable diversity of the State's flora and fauna, examined as individual environments: pine forest uplands, hardwood forests, swamps and marshes. And it's not all boring exhibits—kids can touch live animals, look under microscopes and participate in hands-on activities. Every third Saturday of the month is Feeding Frenzy Saturday, when the Nature Center offers public feedings of its captive snake and raptor populations *(call for schedules).*

Judith W. Freeman Planetarium – The largest planetarium in the New Orleans area, this facility with its 30ft-diameter dome opens the door to the solar system, from the Little Dipper to the Orion Nebula.

Entergy IMAX® Theatre

Canal St. at the river. 504-581-4629 or 800-774-7394. www.auduboninstitute.org/imax. Open year-round Sun–Thu 10am–6pm, Fri & Sat 10am–8pm. Closed Mardi Gras day & Dec 25. Showtimes vary. $8 adults, $5 children (ages 2–12). Combination tickets are available for IMAX and aquarium.

IMAX theaters are now a ubiquitous feature of most large American cities, but that doesn't make them any less cool. Located next to the Aquarium of the Americas, this theater offers a spectacular you-are-there view of subjects ranging from nature to sports to outer space. The comfy facility, with its towering 354ft-high screen, state-of-the-art sound system and  cushy stadium seats, is a great place to escape the crowds and the heat for an hour or two. New Orleans' IMAX is one of only six in the world to offer flat-screen, single-projection, 3-D and high-definition technology. Recent shows have included *Lewis and Clark, Mysteries of Egypt,* and *NASCAR 3D,* which puts you in the driver seat going 200mph—bet it's not just the kids who want to see that one!

City Park★★ For Kids

1 Palm Dr. 504-482-4888. www.neworleanscitypark.com. See Parks and Gardens.

There's plenty of room for kids to run and play in this 1,500-acre park, the fifth-largest urban garden in America. But kids will make a beeline to these two attractions:

Carousel Gardens Amusement Area

City Park at Victory Ave., Mid-City 504-482-4888. www.neworleanscitypark.com/carousel_gardens.php. Hours vary seasonally. Closed Feb. $2 admission; $1/ride or $10 unlimited ride pass.

Who can resist a carousel? Kids of all ages have been riding on City Park's carousel since 1906. It's one of only 100 antique wooden carousels in the country and the last one in Louisiana. The kids may not care that the beautiful hand-carved merry-go-round is listed on the National Register of Historic Places, but anybody with an eye for fine renovation will appreciate this source of local pride. A small amusement park set amid live oaks here entertains the younger set with rides such as a Ferris wheel, bumper cars, a tilt-a-whirl, a roller coaster and two miniature trains that chug around the park.

Storyland

City Park at Victory Ave., Adjacent to Carousel Gardens. 504-482-4888. www.neworleanscitypark.com/storyland_kids.php. Open year-round; hours vary seasonally. $2 (free for children 2 and under).

Come experience your favorite fairy tale. This popular play area, built in the 1950s, includes 26 oversize whimsical storybook exhibits, a Little Mermaid pond and puppet shows *(Wed–Sun; included with admission fee)*. Climb aboard Captain Hook's pirate ship, journey with Pinocchio into the mouth of a whale (a rite of passage for local kids since the park opened) or scamper up Jack & Jill's Hill. Rapunzel presides over the Storyland Players at the Puppet Castle, and special events include a Non-Scary Halloween when storybook characters come to life for little trick-or-treaters. Hands-on craft activities are held regularly in the Mother Goose Circle.

Louisiana Children's Museum

420 Julia St. 504-523-1357. www.lcm.org. Open Jun–mid-Aug Mon–Sat 9:30am–4:30pm,
Sun noon–4:30pm. Rest of the year Tue–Sat 9:30am–4:30pm, Sun noon–4:30pm. $6.

Hands-on learning equals hands-on fun at this spunky children's museum, where kids are encouraged to discover a world of wonder throughout 45,000sq ft of learn-by-doing exhibits. Here you'll find all kinds of fun, geared to children from toddlers to age 12.

Role-playing rules upstairs at Sav-a-Center, a grocery store complete with dairy cases and cashiers; Kid's Cafe, for budding chefs-to-be; and a TV stage set where youngsters can act the part of a news anchor, reporter, director or meteorologist. Older kids favor Team Turtle Training Camp, where video games teach topics like health and fitness; and Art Trek, where would-be artistes can draw, paint and sculpt their own masterpieces.

At Little Port of New Orleans you can track a barge's cargo on an interactive global map, with tugboats and cruise ships vying for space on the make-believe river. Kids can also get charged up by a psychedelic-looking plasma ball, or step inside a giant bubble to see a rainbow of colors.

Kid-Friendly Dining and Dancing

While most music venues are closed to youngsters, Michaul's *(840 St. Charles Ave.; 504-522-5517; www.michauls.com)*, in the Central Business District, is open to all ages. Not only can you get some good Louisiana eats here—fried shrimp and alligator sauce piquante for adults, and a kid's menu for the chicken-finger set), but dancers of all ages are treated to free Cajun dance lessons every week *(Mon–Thu beginning at 6:30pm, Fri & Sat at 7pm)*. Michaul's may not be quite as authentic as the dance halls in **Lafayette**★ *(see Excursions)*, but you'll still experience one heck of a bayou hoedown. And after an evening of dancing, the little darlings are sure to sleep like logs.

Six Flags New Orleans

14mi east of the French Quarter at the junction of I-10 & I-510. 504-253-8100.
www.sixflags.com. Hours vary seasonally. $32.99 adults, $22.99 for children under
48 inches tall; children under 2 get in free.

What had sounded like a good idea—a theme park called Jazzland about 20 minutes outside of New Orleans, ended up being a flop, thanks to a dearth of shade and an overwhelming amount of concrete. Six Flags came to the rescue in 2003, sinking $20 million into the site and transforming it into a rock-'em, sock-'em thrill park, overrun with Looney Tunes and DC Comics characters.

Today the 140-acre park manages to give a Louisiana spin to the attractions, with visitors treated to jazz concerts, an interactive Mardi Gras experience, and adrenalin-pumping rides like the Zydeco Scream, a hair-raising coaster that's true to its name; and the Voodoo Volcano, which does 360-degree flips 50ft in the air.

Here's a Tip:

You can save $1 per ticket if you buy your tickets at any Winn-Dixie supermarket.

If thrill rides aren't for you, there's a live stunt show, the Batman Thrill Spectacular; and a high-stepping musical, State of Rhythm, along with seasonal concerts. Wee ones will enjoy the Looney Tunes Adventure Area, where Bugs Bunny, Daffy Duck and their cronies hang out. New landscaping—they put back the trees!—and water attractions make the park a "cool" destination, even in summer.

Cool Coasters

- In **Batman: The Ride,** you'll travel 50mph and 105ft in the air through a loop of steel.

- **The Jester** puts passengers through a 360-degree vertical loop and a 79ft drop.

- Purists may prefer the **Mega-Zeph,** a 4,000ft-long, 110ft-high wooden monster.

Kids In Kenner

Rivertown Museums

303-519 Williams Blvd., Kenner. 10mi east of New Orleans via I-10. 504-468-7231. www.kenner.la.us/rivertown. Open year-round Tue–Sat 9am–5pm. Multipass to all attractions: $15 adults, $9 children (ages 2–12). Per-museum fee: $3 adults, $2.50 children.

You can easily spend a day in this quaint neighborhood of attractions, which encompasses eight museums, a theater and an art gallery. Located a half-mile from the airport in the suburb of Kenner, the 16-block historic district offers fun for the whole family. Here are a few Rivertown highlights:

Cannes Brûlée Native American Exhibit – *303 Williams Blvd.* The area known as Kenner was once called Cannes Brûlée ("burnt cane" in French) because the Natives used to set fire to the canebreaks to flush out wild game. Today Native Americans demonstrate their folk traditions, rituals, food preparation and crafts here.

Children's Castle – *503 Williams Blvd.* Storytelling, crafts, puppet shows and musical entertainment are featured on a rotating basis at this enchanted castle *(call for schedule)*.

Louisiana Toy Train Museum – *519 Williams Blvd.* All aboard for a trip through an extensive collection of toy trains, working models and visitor-activated trains, including a half-scale locomotive model for kids that includes a caboose, a circus car, and "Dixie Diner," where make-believe meals can be served.

Mardi Gras Museum – *415 Williams Blvd.* It's Mardi Gras all year long at this museum dedicated to the mystery, magic and revelry of the Carnival season. Exhibits span 150 years of history, with films, video clips and memorabilia highlighting king cake traditions, balls and parades. Be sure to catch the float- and costume-making demonstrations.

Space Station Kenner – *409 Williams Blvd.* Budding astronauts will love this full-size NASA International Space Station prototype, where kids can get a first-hand look at daily living and working in space. Explore space spin-off technology with a space robot, touch the four-billion-year-old Gideon Meteorite, and take a walk through the history of space exploration in the 20C.

Must Go: Performing Arts

The very idea of seeking out the performing arts in New Orleans seems redundant—after all, the whole town is a stage, and some of the best performances you'll see anywhere take place on the streets of the French Quarter and in bars all over town. But if your aim is higher on the cultural scale, here are some theatrical venues where the entertainment is more, shall we say, traditional.

Orpheum Theater★

129 University Pl. 504-524-3285. www.orpheumneworleans.com.

This 1921 Beaux-Arts "vertical hall" in the Central Business District provided unobstructed sight lines and great acoustics for the Vaudeville performances it was built to host. In its heyday, the theatre presented the likes of Jack Benny, George Burns, Gracie Allen, and the Marx Brothers. Today the 1,780-seat Orpheum, with its grand vaulted ceiling, Baroque detailing and wonderful acoustics, makes a perfect home for the **Louisiana Philharmonic Orchestra** *(504-523-6530; www.lpomusic.com)*. Formerly the New Orleans Symphony, this musician-owned-and-run organization offers a full season *(Sept–May)* of classics from Bernstein to Tchaikovsky. If you're in town during the summer, check out the philharmonic's free outdoor concerts in City Park—they're a favorite with local music lovers.

Preservation Hall★ – *726 St. Peter St. See Nightlife.*

Le Petit Théâtre du Vieux Carré

616 St. Peter St. 504-522-2081. www.lepetittheatre.com.

Touted as one of the oldest community theaters in the country, Le Petit was founded in the French Quarter in the 1920s by a cadre of art-loving New Orleanians who called themselves the Drawing Room Players. The theater still stages failsafe musicals like *Grease, Forever Plaid* and *Once Upon a Mattress* as well as occasional works by local playwrights. There's also a schedule of seasonal children's productions.

True Brew Theatre

200 Julia St. 504-524-8440. This alternative coffeehouse venue in the Warehouse Arts District serves up lattés in the front and edgy theater in the backroom. The artsy menu ranges from Beatles revues to one-man political satire.

Saenger Theatre

143 N. Rampart St. 504-524-2490. www.saengertheatre.com.

Although the Saenger's glory has faded somewhat since it opened as a 4,000-seat movie
palace in 1927 (it now seats 2,736), the theater's
Greek and Romanesque sculptures and special-
effects ceiling of twinkling stars and moving
clouds are still something to see. It's mostly
touring productions that take the stage now
from October to June (think *Cats, The Pro-
ducers, Phantom of the Opera*), along with the
occasional rock concert. Classic movies like
North by Northwest and *Singin' in the Rain* are projected onto a large screen
here each summer during the annual classic-film series.

Southern Repertory Theatre

*333 Canal St. at The Shops at Canal Place (3rd floor). 504-835-6002.
www.southernrep.com.*

Founded in 1986 to provide an outlet for Southern playwrights, Southern Rep
staged productions in several venues around town before finding a home in
the French Quarter's Shops at Canal Place in 1991. Tennessee Williams, Carson
McCullers and Barrett O'Brien are just of few of the playwrights whose work
has been performed here. A typical season today may touch on works both
dark and comic, as in Dael Orlandersmith's *Yellowman*, an indictment of
racism, and Edward Albee's Tony-award winning comic love story, *The Goat or
Who is Sylvia?* Tickets range from $20 to $30, and there's no assigned seating.

Filming The Big Easy

New Orleans' tattered Southern charm, gorgeous architecture and natural decadence
are the perfect setting for Hollywood storytelling. Here's a Crescent City film for
each of the past six decades. Any surprise that so many are film noir?

Runaway Jury (2003) – This John Grisham court drama stars John Cusak, Dustin
Hoffman and Gene Hackman.

Interview with a Vampire (1994) – Local author Anne Rice's blood-soaked vampire
thriller was filmed on location at **Oak Alley Plantation**★ *(see Excursions/River Road)*
with Brad Pitt as vampire Louis and Tom Cruise as Lestat.

The Big Easy (1987) – Hot music, steamy sex and a crime thriller rolled into one,
starring Dennis Quaid and Ellen Barkin.

Pretty Baby (1978) – Brooke Shields grabbed the pop-culture spotlight in her role as a
child prostitute at a Jazz Age brothel.

Suddenly Last Summer (1960) – Katherine Hepburn stars as a mother coming to terms
with her late son's homosexuality in this flick, based on Tennessee Williams' play
Garden District.

A Streetcar Named Desire (1951) – "Stella!" The Tennessee Williams' classic with
Marlon Brando and Vivian Leigh is the ultimate Big Easy blockbuster.

Must Shop

From kitschy souvenirs to world-class art, New Orleans offers shopping for every taste and budget. Browse the galleries and antique shops of Royal Street, get funky on Magazine Street uptown or peruse the gourmet goodies in the French Market. You're guaranteed to find something you didn't know you needed.

French Quarter★★★

Free of chain stores and fiercely proud of its owner-operated retail sector, this neighborhood boasts fine art galleries, eclectic boutiques and quirky ateliers for everything from hand-made leather masks to hammered-silver jewelry.

Royal Street★★ Rundown

Galleries and antique shops dominate this stretch of Royal Street, with most of the action concentrated in the 10 blocks between Iberville Street and Ursulines Avenue. Here are a few highlights:

Bottom of the Cup Tea Room – *732 Royal St. 504-523-1204 or 800-729-7148. www.madamegstearoom.com.* If you're interested in having your tea leaves or palm read, step inside this occult weigh station, in the seer business since 1929.

Bourbon French Parfums – *815 Royal St. 504-522-4480. www.neworleansperfume.com.* This ooh-la-la French perfumery, housed in an authentic Creole cottage, specializes in custom-blended fragrances, along with imported soaps, lotions and other body delights.

Kabuki Design Studio – *1036 Royal St. 504-523-8004. www.kabukihats.com.* Award-winning local designer Tracy Thomson fashions handmade one-of-a-kind millinery, ranging from formal to whimsical creations.

M.S. Rau Inc. – *630 Royal St. 504-523-5660. www.rauantiques.com.* Shop for French, American and English furniture at this third-generation family business.

Rodrigue Studio – *721 Royal St. 504-581-4244. www.georgerodrigue.com.* Named for the Cajun artist who became world-famous for his portraits of the woebegone blue dog, the gallery features paintings and serigraphs. The artist took his inspiration from the loup-garou, or Cajun ghost dog.

Rumors – *513 Royal St. 504-525-0292.* Shop here for collectible masks, both made locally and imported from Italy.

Three Dog Bakery – *827 Royal St. 504-525-2253. www.threedog.com.* Bring your pooch a selection of "Pawlines" from this pet bakery.

Waldhorn & Adler – *343 Royal St. 504-581-6379.www.waldhornadlers.com.* Max out your credit card at the oldest antique shop in town, where you'll find a wide selection of antique furniture and estate jewelry.

French Market★

1000 block of Decatur St. 504-525-7879. www.frenchmarket.org. Open year-round daily 24hrs a day.

Originally a Choctaw trading post, the French Market dates back to 1791, the oldest documented farmer's market in America. Open 24/7 (individual kiosk hours vary), the market extends from **Café Du Monde** *(see Musts for Fun)* through seven buildings to the Farmers' and Flea Market. The most colorful section contains heaping stands of fresh produce. Then come stalls offering culinary souvenirs, like Cajun spices, pralines and boxes of mix for local favorites like dirty rice and beignets (the latter never tastes like the real thing, so save your money). Organized like a giant swap meet, you can find inexpensive silver jewelry, $5 sunglasses, and all kinds of questionable items made from alligator hide. Try your hand at bargaining—depending on the shop owner's mood and how much you're planning to buy, you might get a good deal.

Artist's Market

1228 Decatur St. 504-913-0987 or 504-701-7388. Open year-round daily 10am–6pm.

Steps away from the French Market, this artist's cooperative is run by a talented crew of local artists who make ceramics, art-to-wear, garden ornaments, Mardi Gras masks and hammered copper and silver jewelry. Decidedly non-commercial, this is a great place to pick up an interesting piece of wall art to remind you of your trip.

Decatur Street

This prime tourist area by the riverfront has some places worth checking out.

Aunt Sally's Praline Shop – *810 Decatur St. 504-524-3373. www.auntsallys.com.* Brown sugar, butter and pecans are the holy trinity that make Louisiana pralines so darn good. This shop makes the treats fresh daily in their open kitchen. Take home a box for your sweetheart—or the kids.

Louisiana Music Factory – *210 Decatur St. 504-586-1094. www.louisianamusicfactory.com.* This is

the place to come for the local music you can't get at home, including an outstanding selection of zydeco, blues and traditional brass bands. Stop by on Saturday, when as many as three local music acts stage an in-store performance. The Factory is the unofficial music headquarters of the New Orleans Jazz and Heritage Festival.

Magazine Street★★

For general information, call the Magazine Street Merchant Association, 800-387-8924 or 504-455-1224. www.magazinestreet.com.

Stretching six miles parallel to the Mississippi River from Canal Street to Audubon Park, Magazine Street travels from the Central Business District all the way through the Warehouse Arts District and the Garden District to Uptown. Originally named for a warehouse that Spanish Governor Miro built to house Kentucky tobacco and other exports, this funky street is an antidote to the typical mall experience. Clusters of shops are interspersed with residential properties, a down-to-earth mix of renovated warehouses and 19C shops selling housewares, pottery, period furniture, clothing, books, glassware, toys, china, soaps and jewelry.

Magazine Street is the ideal spot for a leisurely walkabout, with plenty of coffee shops, cafes and restaurants to provide refreshment for the tired shopper. Take the Magazine Street bus from Canal Street, or to go further uptown, take the **St. Charles Streetcar★★** *(see Musts for Fun)* and walk one block towards the river to Magazine. You'll find the heaviest concentration of shops in the seven-block stretch between Audubon Park and Felicity Street.

Mercantile Magazine Street

Crescent City Farmers Market – *700 Magazine St. 504-861-5898. www.crescentcityfarmersmarket.org. Open year-round Sat 8am–noon.* More than 50 vendors proffer farm-fresh produce, seafood and flowers at this friendly little market every Saturday. The same local purveyors supply some of the city's best restaurants, including Bayona, Commander's Palace and Chateaubriand *(see Must Eat).*

Jax Brewery – *600 Decatur St. Central Business District 504-566-7245. www.jacksonbrewery.com. Open year-round Mon–Sat 9am–8pm, Sun 10am–7pm.* This 1891 brew house is now a riverfront mall with more than 50 shops and restaurants including Virgin Megastore, Cajun Clothing Company, and Chico's. A museum devoted to the brewery, which closed in the mid-1970s, is open to the public free of charge.

The Living Room – *3324 Magazine St. 504-891-8251. www.magazinestreet.com. Second location: 927 Royal St., French Quarter. 504-595-8860.* Retro home furnishings and accessories here cater to the anti-Pottery Barn set. Don't forget to shake paws with the resident dogs, Louise and Earl.

Lucullus – *3932 Magazine St. 504-894-0500. www.magazinestreet.com. Second location: 610 Chartres St., French Quarter. 504-528-9620.* This fascinating shop specializes in culinary antiques, from antique china and silver settings to rustic farmhouse implements and accoutrements for the ritualistic serving of absinthe (which was banned in 1912).

Mignon Faget – *3801 Magazine St. 504-891-2005. www.mignonfaget.com.* Named for an award-winning local artist, this shop specializes in jewelry inspired by symbols synonymous with New Orleans, from a gumbo necklace dripping with shrimp, crab and okra charms to king cake pendant earrings and French fleur-de-lis designs.

Ms. Spratts – *4537 Magazine St. 504-891-0063. www.magazinestreet.com.* Progressive fashion and eclectic accessories for the big, beautiful woman, ranging in sizes from 1X to 5X.

New Orleans Centre – *1400 Poydras St. 504-568-0000.* Located in the shadow of the Superdome, this three-story shopping mall is connected to the Hyatt Regency and offers the likes of national retailers Macys, Lord and Taylor and The Gap.

Riverwalk Marketplace – *1 Poydras St. 504-522-1555. www.riverwalkmarketplace.com.* The same developers who brought you South Street Seaport in New York City and Harborplace in Baltimore designed this shopping and dining complex with 140 retail stores and restaurants. Abercrombie & Fitch, Ann Taylor Loft and Structure are a few of the familiar names.

The Shops at Canal Place – *333 Canal St. 504-522-9200. www.theshopsatcanalplace.com.* Anchored by Saks Fifth Avenue, this upscale shopping center includes Gucci, BCBG, Williams-Sonoma and Brooks Brothers. A few non-chain stores are included in the mix, most notably the RHINO Gallery—for Right Here In New Orleans, which is where its unique mix of crafts and art jewelry is made *(504-523-7945; www.rhinocrafts.com).*

Two Chicks – *2917 Magazine St. 504-896-8855. www.magazinestreet.com.* Offbeat and whimsical home accessories keep company with handmade ceramics and papier-mâché bowls at this inviting emporium of all that's cool.

Just name that tune—blues, jazz, folk-rock, funk, zydeco. New Orleans boasts some of the best nightlife of any city in America. If you have the energy, you can see two and three great musical acts a night, on any night of the week—even Monday. If you leave the French Quarter at night, keep in mind that your cab fare buys you some of the most authentic tunes in town.

Preservation Hall★

726 St. Peter St., French Quarter. 504-523-8939 or 800-785-5772. www.preservationhall.com.

It may not look like much at first glance, but this private home turned performance hall is still "where you'll find all the greats" in the words of Louis Armstrong. Opened in 1961, Preservation Hall was founded to give local musicians a place to play New Orleans jazz. Those bench seats may be anything but comfortable and the setting may be a bit rustic, but Preservation Hall reigns as a mecca for fans of traditional New Orleans-style jazz.

Half-hour sets begin at 8:30pm and end at midnight, but folks start lining up early to get a seat—the trick to avoiding the line is to get there either just as the doors open or later in the evening. Bring the kids and prepare for a rollicking good time—this is one of the few family-friendly jazz venues in town.

Apple Barrel Inn

609 Frenchmen St., Faubourg Marigny. 504-949-9399.

This smoky neighborhood hole-in-the-wall is known for its cheap, strong drinks, friendly crowd and regular appearances by cowboy-hat-clad roots/blues artist Coco Robichaux.

Cover Charges

Cover charges vary wildly at New Orleans clubs, depending on the band and the venue. Whether there is a cover or not, it's standard practice for most bands to pass the hat after each set, or keep a donation box on the bandstand—give generously, since musicians are a notoriously underpaid group. You'll rarely find a cover charge on Bourbon Street, but expect inflated drink prices to compensate. Don't be shy about counter-offering on a cover charge, especially if you're with a group—in New Orleans, just about everything is negotiable.

Café Brasil

2100 Chartres St., Faubourg Marigny. 504-949-0851.

The crowd spills out onto the street on any given night at Café Brasil, the pioneer of the burgeoning club scene in the Marigny. A variety of music is featured almost every night, from Latin and Caribbean, to R&B and acid jazz, attracting a young and trendy crowd. There's a big dance floor, but on a hot night, you'll have just as much fun dancing in the street.

Circle Bar

1032 St. Charles St., Warehouse Arts District. 504-588-2616.

Calling all lounge lizards: this tiny spot will soon become your home away from home. With its neon K&B drugstore sign on the ceiling, slightly shabby décor and excellent jukebox, Circle Bar is a hipster's paradise. It also attracts an eclectic array of life artists, from surf duos to local singer-songwriters and jazz trios, who tuck into an impossibly small bandstand and proceed to rock out.

Donna's Bar & Grill

800 N. Rampart St., French Quarter. 504-596-6914.

It's best to take a cab to this brassy music mecca on the northern edge of the Quarter, across from Tremé and Louis Armstrong Park. Donna's is one of the best places to experience both veteran brass bands like Tremè and Olympia and younger musicians fueling the revival of the brass-band experience, with groups like the Rebirth, the Chosen Few, the Little Rascals and the Soul Rebels tearing things up onstage.

d.b.a.

618 Frenchmen St., Faubourg Marigny. 504-942-3731.
www.drinkgoodstuff.com/no.

The New Orleans outpost of this chic New York club isn't as gritty as most great bars in town, but it does offer an array of good live music, featuring local acts like Walter "Wolfman" Washington, Theresa Andersson and Cyril Neville. The beer list tops 160 labels—the best variety in town. Dark wood and low lighting make for an intimate vibe.

FQB

921 Canal St. in the Ritz Carlton, French Quarter.
504-524-1331. www.ritzcarlton.com.

Tucked inside the Ritz-Carlton hotel, FQB (which stands for French Quarter Bar) is a hot spot for grown-ups. The draw is house bandleader Jeremy Davenport, a protégé of Harry Connick Jr., with a Sinatra-esque set of pipes and a mean set of chops on the trumpet. A revolving guest list of local musicians stop by regularly to sit in with the band.

Funky Butt

714 N. Rampart St., French Quarter. 504-558-0872. www.funkybutt.com.

Named in honor of a century-old tune associated with local jazz musician Buddy "King" Bolden, the Funky Butt is a comfortable place to hear a litany of great performers, from the Wild Magnolias, the best-known troupe of Mardi Gras Indians, to local sons Nicholas Payton and Trombone Shorty. The ambience is down-home and the Louisiana-style comfort food is cheap and delish.

Funky Pirate

727 Bourbon St., French Quarter. 504-523-1960.

One of the best of the Bourbon Street clubs, this cozy blues venue features a dynamite house band—Big Al Carson and the Blues Masters—and a lethal house drink, the Hand Grenade, a potent mix of rum and vodka served in neon-green plastic. Like most clubs on Bourbon Street, expect high drink prices to offset the lack of a cover charge.

House of Blues

225 Decatur St., French Quarter. 504-529-2583. www.hob.com.

There's no getting around the corporate-franchise feel to this national entertainment chain, which takes up a half-block on Decatur. Skip the gospel brunch (it's overpriced) and stay for the headliners, who benefit from a music room with good sight lines and great acoustics. The chain's buying power delivers big names like out-of-towners Los Lobos and Nanci Griffith along with local faves the Neville Brothers and Galactic.

Howlin' Wolf

828 S. Peters St., Warehouse Arts District. 504-522-9653. www.howlin-wolf.com.

This locally owned and operated club is one of the best and biggest in town, host to such high-quality indie rock acts as Frank Black, the Jon Spencer Blues Explosion, and Iris DeMent. The music isn't limited to rock—you're just as likely to see Rickie Lee Jones or local heroes, The Funky Meters, on stage.

Le Chat Noir

715 St. Charles Ave., Central Business District. 504-581-5812. www.cabaretlechatnoir.com.

Life is a cabaret at this St. Charles venue, which plays host to all kinds of alternative productions, from small musicals to tango lessons and lively political repartee. Drag shows are not unheard of, and original musicals, like the Black and White Blues, about working in the New Orleans restaurant business, are especially fun. Be aware that $6 is added to the price of your ticket for a drink.

Lion's Den

2655 Gravier St., Mid-City. 504-821-3745.

Co-owned by local R&B diva Irma Thomas, this Mid-City dive is always worth the cab ride, whether Thomas is in residence or not. She puts on quite a show, and is a true mistress of the double-entendre blues song. If you're lucky, Irma may just be serving her famous red beans and rice.

Maple Leaf Bar

8316 Oak St., Uptown. 504-866-9359.

A tin roof, a small dance floor and a line-up of great funk, Cajun, R&B and blues music describes one of the city's best music experiences. Walter "Wolfman" Washington is a regular, and if Beausoleil or the ReBirth Brass Band is playing, you won't have a better time anywhere in town.

Mermaid Lounge

1102 Constance St., Warehouse Arts District. 504-524-4747.

This funky gem is off the beaten track, where a series of one-way streets and a cul-de-sac location keep anybody but serious music lovers away. The cramped, building welcomes eclectic music from the Cajun waltzes of the Grammy-nominated Hackberry Ramblers to the latest hard-core grunge. Locals dodge the cover by standing out on the sidewalk, where the acoustics are just fine.

Mid-City Lanes Rock-N-Bowl

4133 S. Carrollton Ave., Mid-City. 504-482-3133. www.rockandbowl.com.

It doesn't get any more authentic than this club smack in the middle of a strip-mall bowling alley, the best place in town for zydeco and *the* place to buy a bar t-shirt to add to your collection. Stand-outs include Geno Delafose, C.J. Chenier, Anders Osborne, and The Iguanas. The dance floor is always crowded, the music is ear-splittingly loud, and climate control is non-existent—which is exactly why you won't want to leave.

Mother-In-Law Lounge

1500 N. Claiborne Ave., Tremé. 504-947-1078. www.kdoe.com.

Ernie K-Doe, the voice behind 1961 novelty hit Mother-In-Law, is gone, but certainly not forgotten. His widow, Antoinette, has created a shrine to the man who billed himself as "Emperor the Universe." You have to knock to gain entry to this quirky bar, and a cab is a must. Claiborne Avenue, in the shadow of I-10, was once an African-American version of Bourbon Street, but fell onto hard times after the highway bisected the neighborhood.

Mulate's

201 Julia St., Warehouse Arts District. 504-522-1492 or 800-854-9149. www.mulates.com.

Although under different ownership from the original Cajun country location, Mulate's in the trendy Warehouse Arts District is your best bet for Cajun music and dancing. Bands like Lee Benoit, La Touche and Jay Cormier burn it up with swamp boogie music. If you work up an appetite, you can get a decent gumbo or étoufée from the kitchen.

Oz

800 Bourbon St., French Quarter. 504-592-8200 or 877-599-8200.
www.ozneworleans.com.

This two-level disco is the place to see and be seen for the (mostly) young gay crowd, with featured calendar-boy revues and female impersonators geared to whip the crowd into a frenzy. The music features house and dance mixes, with a great laser-light show, and the occasional go-go boy atop the bar.

Palm Court Jazz Café

1204 Decatur St., French Quarter. 504-525-0200. www.palmcourtjazzcafe.com.

An elegant venue for traditional jazz, the Palm Court is a more refined place to catch some of the same acts that frequent Preservation Hall. Music is featured Wednesday though Sunday, with the emphasis on classic jazz. Take note of the collection of jazz records for sale in a back alcove. Make reservations for dinner—the Creole food is excellent—and stay for the duration.

Pete Fountain's Club

2 Poydras St., in the Hilton New Orleans Riverside, Central Business District.
504-561-0500.

You'll need a reservation to pull up a red-velvet seat at Pete Fountain's plush New Orleans home base in the Central Business District, where he plays three times a week when he's in town. Fountain's style of Dixieland is so synonymous with New Orleans music that he was immortalized (with a blue dog) on the official Jazz Fest poster a few years ago. Call to check on the performance schedule as Pete's frequently on tour.

Praline Connection Gospel & Blues Hall

907 S. Peters St., Warehouse Arts District. 504-523-3973.
www.pralineconnection.com.

Unlike the Praline Connection in the Marigny, this location has a stage for live music and 9,000sq ft of elbow room. You'll still be able to order some mighty fine fried chicken and étoufée, and you can dance it off to the sounds of live blues and jazz. Make time for the gospel brunch on Sunday—it's the real deal.

R Bar

1431 Royal St., in the Royal Street Inn, Faubourg Marigny. 504-948-7499.
www.royalstreetinn.com.

This funky local hangout attracts an offbeat mix
of artists, wannabe artists, inebriated intellectuals
and musicians who stop by after their set—a kind
of dysfunctional Cheers. There's a great alt-rock
juke box, a large selection of imported beers,
friendly bartenders, and on Mondays, you can get
a haircut and a shot for $10.

Snug Harbor

626 Frenchmen St., Faubourg Marigny. 504-949-0696. www.snugjazz.com.

Snug Harbor is a must for both food and music. The menu is American and the
upstairs jazz venue, while cramped, is the place to see Ellis Marsalis (patriarch
of the Marsalis clan) on a Friday night. Contemporary jazz, blues and R&B
combos are the usual fare, with Charmaine Neville another regular you won't
want to miss.

Spotted Cat

623 Frenchmen St., Faubourg Marigny. 504-943-3887.

A tiny little club in the Marigny, the Spotted Cat never charges a cover, yet it
delivers some of the best local music, from brassy jazz combos to acoustic
strummers. Traditional jazz is featured regularly, and on Mondays and Fridays
the New Orleans Jazz Vipers offer a fresh take on classic jazz. It's a great place
to escape the Frenchmen Street madness.

Tipitina's

501 Napoleon Ave., Uptown. 504-895-8477. www.tipitinas.com.

Named for a song by the legendary Professor Longhair, Tips is *the* quintessen-
tial New Orleans club, even though its luster has dulled over the years, due
to increased competition in the marketplace. While it may not have the
booking muscle of years gone by (Taj Mahal, Dr. John and Bonnie Raitt all
played here), it's still a reliable spot for local acts, brass bands, and touring
alt-rock and roots acts. Go Sunday night for Cajun fun with Bruce Daigrepont
and free red beans and rice.

Vaughan's Lounge

4229 Dauphine St., Bywater. 504-947-5562.

Thursday night is the time to take a short cab ride from the Quarter to this
homey bar, where Kermit Ruffin, the local trumpet player often likened to a
young Louis Armstrong, holds court. His band is called the Barbecue Swingers, a
reference to both their swinging groove, and the barbecue Kermit usually cooks
up before the show. The bartender will call you a cab when you're ready to leave.

The Big Easy can be tough on the body—between the walking by day, dancing by night, and overall journey into excess, after a few days you'll likely need a little pampering. Tuckered tourists and local movers and shakers alike line up for the latest skincare and massage treatments at these tony spas.

Belladonna

2900 Magazine St. 504-891-4393. www.belladonnadayspa.com.

This fragrant Garden District day spa brings the serenity of the East to its approach to beauty with Jamu ancient Indonesian spa rituals. A blend of exotic ingredients and Indonesian traditions are used for a series of treatments like Be Purified, Be Royal, and Be Invigorated. Indigenous island ingredients such as mineral clay are used to purify, and sea salt, flower petals and oils accomplish a gentle exfoliation. A paste of clove, ginger and dried flowers is applied to sooth both mind and body. Ahhh.

Bliss Day Spa & Shop

200 Metairie Rd., Metairie. 504-828-1997. www.dayspbliss.com.

Located in the suburb of Metairie, this intimate full-service salon is known for its signature "Day of Bliss" treatment—a full day of pampering with a 60-minute massage, a facial, a manicure and a pedicure, with lunch thrown in. Give your guy a "Bliss Him Out" package that includes a full-body massage and a reflexology treatment. You won't want to leave without purchasing some products from Dr. Mary Lupo's great skincare line.

Bodyjoys Day Spa & Salon

3423 St. Charles Ave. 504-895-4400 or 800-331-7812. www.bodyjoys.com.

An extensive array of spa services fills the menu at luxurious Bodyjoys, where a highly skilled and certified staff serves up everything from a fantasy tan (a sunless tanning application that lasts up to two weeks) to a sea-salt body scrub. Stress-busting combo packages are the way to go.

Earthsavers Relaxation Spa & Store

434 Chartres St. 504-581-4999. www.earthsaversonline.com.

True to their name, Earthsavers features a signature product line that is made with fine natural ingredients and contains no animal by-products or mineral oils (and, of course, they're not tested on animals). Services at this holistic French Quarter day spa are low-tech and unhurried; facials, body work, manicures, pedicures, reflexology and waxing are all available. The spa's series of wellness seminars promotes their philosophy that just "feeling ok isn't good enough."

Miss Celie's Spa Orleans

914 N Rampart St. 504-522-7288 or 800-522-7288.www.spaorleans.com.

Located in the Olde Victorian Inn, on the northern edge of the French Quarter near Treme, Miss Celie's is not your average day spa. Not only can you get a past-life-regression massage, but your pet can have a relaxing massage as well—all pets are welcome. The spa is named for Miss Celie Brune, a Creole woman who catered to New Orleans' socialites at her *Maison de Beauté* back in the 1830s. Modern-day pampering is de rigueur, with lots of extra touches to make you feel like royalty.

Pampered Soul & Body Day Spa

4826 Magazine St. 504-895-5333. www.pamperedsoulandbody.com.

Your spirit gets as much TLC as your body at this Magazine Street day spa, which promotes healing rituals like Jin Shin Jyutsu, based on the Japanese philosophy of channeling energy; and Reiki, a treatment system that works on energy meridians along the body. Of course, they also offer aromatherapy and therapeutic massage. If a seaweed facial isn't your thing, standard spa services like manicures/pedicures, waxing and hair cut/coloring are also available.

Riverside Relaxation Spa

116 Carondelet St. 504-581-3033. www.riversidespa.com.

This unpretentious, but well appointed spa in the Central Business District offers warm and professional therapists and a variety of specialty treatments, including hot-stone massage and foot reflexology. The hot chocolate-mint pedicure is so delicious you'll be tempted to suck your toes.

The Spa at the Ritz Carlton

921 Canal St. First level, French Quarter entrance. 504 524-1331 or 800-241-3333. www.ritzcarlton.com.

By far the grandest spa in town, the Spa at the Ritz is decked out with draped chandeliers, marble fountains and other touches of beau-monde elegance. Signature treatments include the 70-minute Essence of Magnolia massage, which begins with a magnolia-scented bath followed by a relaxing Swedish massage. The magnolia sugar scrub will leave your skin polished and glowing, and the synchronized Four-Handed Massage, performed by two therapists, will lull you into a state of transcendent bliss. Robes are acceptable attire at the mezzanine-level spa cafe.

If you can tear yourself away from New Orleans for a while, within a couple of hours' drive of the city you'll discover vestiges of the antebellum South along the River Road, the rustic charm—and fabulous food—of Cajun Country, and the white sands of the Gulf Coast beaches.

River Road★★

Northwest of New Orleans via US-90 West. Visitor information: 888-225-4003 or www.louisianatravel.com.

A trip to the New Orleans area just isn't complete without an excursion along River Road for a look at one of the finest collections of antebellum plantation homes in the South. By car, you can get from New Orleans to the River Road, which hugs both banks of the Mississippi for 120mi between New Orleans and Baton Rouge, within 90 minutes (unfortunately, the drive itself is not the most scenic, as the riverbanks have been marred by a glut of oil and chemical plants). If you don't have a car, your hotel concierge can arrange a plantation tour that includes transportation.

Getting Around the River Road

There are roadways on both sides of the river, including sections of several state highways—notably Highway 18 on the west bank and Highway 44 on the east bank. Route numbers change along the way, but if you keep to the levees, you won't get lost. The Hale Boggs Bridge (I-310), the Veteran's Memorial Bridge (Hwy. 641) and the Sunshine Bridge (Hwy. 70) allow you to cross between the east and west banks.

Plantation Life – Beginning in the early 18C, Louisiana's French colonial government encouraged agricultural development along the river by granting plots of land to wealthy individuals, who established plantations and contained the river's waters behind man-made embankments called levees. Sugarcane, cotton, indigo and rice thrived in the rich soil of the Mississippi River floodplain, providing planters with fortunes to support their extravagant lifestyle. By the early 19C, some 2,000 plantations were flourishing in the region.

Large homes built by slave labor formed the heart of most plantations. Architects borrowed elements from West Indies architecture in trying to adapt the French-Creole houses to Louisiana's hot, humid climate: opposing doors and windows promoted air circulation; steeply pitched ceilings with dormers drew heat upward and aided ventilation; broad galleries served as outdoor "rooms; detached kitchens prevented the spread of fire; and thick walls of *bousillage*, a mixture of mud, moss and horsehair, shielded interior rooms from the heat.

Most of the main entrances faced the river, to welcome visitors arriving by boat. Many homes incorporated a separate wing called a *garconnière,* a kind of latter-day bachelor's pad, where the young men of the family would live once they turned 15. After the Civil War, many of the Creole homes were updated with the classical ornamentation typical of the Greek Revival style that was in fashion at the time.

Fast Facts: Louisiana Plantation Life

- Some of Louisiana's most successful planters were free African Americans, who owned more property than free blacks in any other state.

- In 1860 there were 472 free black Louisianans, whose average real-estate holdings were worth more than $10,000. Compare this to South Carolina, home to 162 free blacks who owned less than $5,000 in real estate in 1860.

- Three out of every 10 free black estate owners in Louisiana were women.

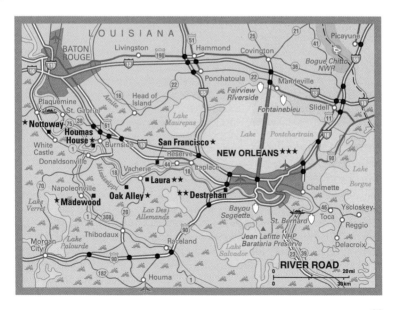

East Bank

The sights below are listed from south to north.

Destrehan★★

22mi northwest of New Orleans. 13034 River Rd., in Destrehan. Take US-90 West to Hwy. 48. 985-764-9315. www.destrehanplantation.org. Open year-round daily 9am–4pm. Closed major holidays. $10.

Completed in 1790 as the heart of a 6,000-acre indigo plantation, Destrehan is considered the oldest documented plantation in the Mississippi Valley. In 1810 the French Colonial-style manor was purchased by Jean Noel Destrehan and his wife, Celeste de Logny (daughter of the home's original owner), who added two wings to the house to make room for their 14 children. Destrehan, who, along with his brother-in-law Etienne de Boré, perfected the process of granulating sugar, replanted the acreage with sugar cane. A later owner remodeled the residence in the then-popular Greek Revival style. Destrehan was restored in the 1970s and furnished with 19C antiques and decorative arts, including items owned by members of the Destrehan family.

San Francisco★

44mi northwest of New Orleans on Hwy. 44, in Reserve. 985-535-2341. www.sanfranciscoplantation.org. Open Mar–Oct daily 9:30am–5:30pm (last tour at 4:40pm). Rest of the year daily 9:30am–4pm. $10.

When you first see San Francisco, with its ornate latticework, scrolled cornices and captain's walk, you might think you're looking at a steamboat. In fact, the mansion's distinctive style has been dubbed "Steamboat Gothic," for its resemblance to the riverboats passing on the Mississippi. Built in 1856, San Francisco is authentically restored to c.1860, when the sugarcane plantation was at the height of its prosperity, and the wife of owner Antoine Valsin undertook a lavish redecoration. Her excess prompted Valsin to comment that the house left him sans fruscin, or "without a cent," which was later anglicized to San Francisco.

Houmas House★

73mi northwest of New Orleans. 40136 Hwy. 942, in Burnside. 504-891-9494. www.houmashouse.com. Open year-round daily 9am–5pm. $20.

You may recognize Houmas House as the setting for the 1965 film *Hush, Hush Sweet Charlotte,* starring Bette Davis. Once part of a 20,000-acre sugarcane plantation, the 21-room mansion actually consists of two different structures: a modest four-room c.1790 residence and a stately 1840 Greek Revival mansion. The latter was built for John Smith Preston, a son-in-law of Revolutionary War hero Wade Hampton, who purchased the property in 1812. Inside, you'll find a lovely freestanding spiral staircase and an extensive collection of period antiques belonging to the current owner.

West Bank

The sights below are listed from north to south.

Nottoway Plantation★

80mi northwest of New Orleans. 30970 Hwy. 405, in White Castle. 225-545-2730 or 866-527-6884. www.nottoway.com. Tours year-round daily 9am–5pm. No tours Dec 25. $10.

This ornate white mansion (1859) is the largest plantation home in the South, a fanciful mix of Greek Revival and Italianate styles. Designed by Henry Howard for Virginia sugarcane magnate John Hampden Randolph, the 53,000sq ft house now operates as a restaurant and inn. It's well worth a stop to tour the house, or to have a meal—the 250-seat restaurant serves lunch and dinner daily.

Oak Alley★

61mi northwest of New Orleans. 3645 Hwy. 18, in Vacherie. 225-265-215 or 800-442-5539. www. oakalleyplantation.com. Tours year-round daily 9am–5:30pm. Rest of the year 9am–5pm. $10.

Named for the gracious quarter-mile-long **allee**★ of 28 live oaks that approaches it on the river side, the columned Greek revival mansion was completed in 1839 as the centerpiece of a flourishing sugarcane plantation. (The trees predate the house

by more than a century.) Costumed docents give tours of the interior, which is furnished with period antiques. Located in a 19C cottage near the mansion, the **Oak Alley Restaurant** serves Cajun fare at lunch. Lodging is available in a cluster of cottages on the grounds.

Laura Plantation★★

50mi northwest of New Orleans. 2247 Hwy. 18 Vacherie. 225-265-7690. www.lauraplantation.com. Visit by guided tour only year-round daily 9:30am–5pm. $10.

Fascinating guided tours of this colorful raised Creole cottage (1805) focus on the Creole culture of New Orleans and the lower Mississippi Valley. The women of the Du Parc and Locoul families operated the sugarcane plantation for 84 years, until Laura Locoul sold a portion of the lands to the German-born Wauguespack family. Laura's private diaries and ledgers provide an insightful glimpse into the inner workings of a plantation business.

The 12 historic outbuildings on-site include original slave cabins where, in the 1870s, the West African folktales of Br'er Rabbit (later published by Joel Chandler Harris) were first recorded.

Madewood★

4250 Hwy. 308, 2mi south of Napoleonville. 504-369-7151. www.madewood.com. 13 rooms. Designed by noted Louisiana architect Henry Howard, this stately c.1846 National Historic Landmark exemplifies the area's Greek Revival architecture. You can experience Madewood's Southern ambience by staying here, since the mansion is now a B&B. Rates for a double room *($259)*, include a wine and cheese reception, a set-menu candlelight dinner, and a full plantation breakfast. If you're not a guest here, you can tour Madewood daily from 10am–4pm *(no tours Jan 1, Thanksgiving Day & Dec 25).*

Cajun Country★

*West of New Orleans via I-10. Visitor information: Lafayette Convention &
Visitors Commission, 337-232-3737 or 800-346-1958; www.lafayettetravel.com.*

Hop in your car and tune the radio to 101 FM (KBON)—you're headed to Cajun
Country. Officially nicknamed Acadiana, this rough triangle of 22 Louisiana
parishes (in other states, they're called counties), extends from St. Landry
Parish to the Gulf of Mexico. With Lafayette at its heart, Acadiana embraces
St. Martinville, New Iberia, Abbeville and Eunice, among other towns, which all
share a history and culture that's unique in America.

The Acadians' Story

Between 1632 and 1651, approximately 18,000 French colonists migrated to the
southeastern coast of Canada in a region of Nova Scotia they named *Acadie*
(Acadia). Theirs was a peaceful agricultural society based on a strong Catholic
faith, deep love of family, and respect for their modest land holdings. The
community was largely isolated from European culture until 1713, when the
French ceded their claims to Nova Scotia to the British under terms of the
Treaty of Utrecht.

The treaty gave the Acadians the choice of becoming British subjects or
leaving the territory. Taking an oath of allegiance to Britain would mean giving
up their religion and possibly having to bear arms against fellow Frenchmen;
leaving the area would deprive the Acadians of their rich farmlands. Thus the
Acadians claimed neutrality, agreeing to take the oath of allegiance if they
were exempted from military service. At first the British governor agreed, but
in 1775 Governor Charles Lawrence recanted and delivered an ultimatum to

the Acadians—take an
unqualified oath of
allegiance or be removed
from Nova Scotia. When
the Acadians refused,
Lawrence issued his
Deportation Order. Over
the next eight years,
14,600 Acadians were
forced to leave their
homes in what became
known as *le grand
dérangement*.

Evangeline

In 1847 American poet **Henry Wadsworth Longfellow** (1807–1882) wrote an epic
account about two lovers, Evangeline and Gabriel, who were separated on their wedding day during the deportation of the Acadians. Remnants of this tragic tale live on
in **St. Martinville** *(15mi southeast of Lafayette via Rtes. 90 & 96)*. The **Evangeline Oak,**
which anchors Evangeline Boulevard just south of St. Martin Square, is said to be the
site of the brief reunion of the real couple who inspired Longfellow's poem.

Villages were burned, families were separated, and more than half of the Acadians lost their lives. In 1784 the King of Spain agreed to allow the remaining Acadians to settle in southern Louisiana. Receiving a less-than-warm welcome from the French aristocrats in New Orleans, most of the Acadians headed west, settling along the bayous of south central and southwestern Louisiana.

Distinguished by their lively music, distinctive cuisine and open hospitality, Cajuns welcome visitors to join their enthusiastic pursuit of a good time (the word Cajun derives from the French *les Acadiens*). Fiddles and accordions set feet flying in local dance halls; rice-stuffed boudin (BOO-dan) pork sausage, and sweet, succulent crawfish—the state crustacean—appear on local tables; and Cajun French, a local dialect that evolved over the centuries in this isolated outpost, is still as prevalent as English in these parts.

Shadows-on-the-Teche★★

317 E. Main St., New Iberia. 318-369-6446. www.shadowsontheteche.org. Open year-round daily 9am–4:30pm. Closed Jan 1, Thanksgiving Day & Dec 25. $7.

Moss-draped live oaks create a play of light and shadow over this elegant brick Classical Revival mansion, which borders sluggish Bayou Teche. Shadows was built in 1834 as part of a 158-acre plantation by sugarcane planter David Weeks. Unfortunately, Weeks died in August 1834, never having lived in the house. The residence remained in the Weeks family for four generations before it was deeded to the National Trust for Historic Preservation.

Inside, the floorplan is typical of Louisiana's colonial days; it has exterior staircases, wide outdoor galleries and opposing windows and doors designed to

enhance circulation in the muggy bayou climate. Nearly every item in the house is original, including fine Federal and Empire-style furniture from New York and Philadelphia, Staffordshire china, and family portraits. Framed by boxwood hedges, two acres of gardens color the grounds year-round with azaleas, camellias, magnolias and crape myrtle.

Festivals Acadiens

If you can, plan your visit to Cajun Country around Lafayette's Festivals Acadiens, held the third weekend in September every year in Girard Park. The three-day series of free festivals celebrates Cajun culture with music, crafts, folkways, and a feast from the bayou—think shrimp jambalaya, crawfish beignets, homemade boudin sausage. "Fais do-do," as they say in Cajun Country (put the kids to bed and party hearty)!

Lafayette★

135mi west of New Orleans via I-10. Visitor Center at 1400 N.W. Evangeline Thruway. 337-232-3737 or 800-346-1958. www.lafayettetravel.com.

Founded in 1836 as Vermilionville and renamed in 1844 to honor the French Revolutionary War hero the Marquis de Lafayette, Lafayette is the hub of Acadiana, and makes an excellent base for exploring the region. A flurry of downtown development has fueled the city's growth, including three new sites: a $16.7-million convention center that opened in 2002; the first phase of the University of Louisiana at Lafayette's 39,000sq ft **University Art Museum** *(710 E. St. Mary Blvd.; 337-482-5326; www.louisiana.edu/UAM)*; and **The Acadiana Center for the Arts** *(corner of Vermilion & Jefferson Sts.; 337-233-7060; www.acadianaartscouncil.org)*, due to open in late 2004 with a state-of-the-art theater for dance, music and drama.

Acadian Cultural Center★★ – *501 Fisher Rd., Lafayette. 337-232-0789. www.nps.gov/jela. Open year-round daily 8am–5pm. Closed Mardi Gras day & Dec 25.* Operated by the Jean Lafitte National Historical Park and Preserve, the center is an excellent place to begin your foray into Cajun Country. A

series of displays focuses on various aspects of Cajun life in Louisiana, highlighting traditional farming, building techniques, language, clothing, music, crafts and more. A 40-minute video, *Echoes of Acadia*, dramatizes the Acadian expulsion from Nova Scotia.

Cajun Cuisine

Rooted in traditions more than two centuries old, Cajun food harkens back to the simple foodways of agrarian France, brought to Louisiana by Acadian farmers and adapted with local ingredients. Rice, one of the major crops of Southwest Louisiana, is a staple in the Cajun diet, finding its way into boudin sausage, countless stews, or just plain old rice topped with thick meat gravy—a classic Cajun dish. Crawfish, also called crayfish, mudbugs and crawdads in Louisiana parlance, are a must for every festival, summer party and outdoor picnic. Crawfish turn red like lobsters when they're boiled, and are best eaten with your fingers. Along with shrimp and oysters from local waters, crawfish form the base for many regional dishes: **étoufée**, or smothered, in a vegetable-laden sauce; simmered with rice, tomatoes, meats and spices in **jambalaya**; and stewed with okra (a green pod vegetable brought by slaves from Africa) in rich **gumbo**. Whatever else you do while you're in Cajun Country, you won't go home hungry.

Acadian Village ★ – *200 Greenleaf Dr., Lafayette. 337-981-4034. www.acadianvillage.org.* You'll get a good feel for how Acadian settlers lived on the bayou in the mid 19C at this rustic re-created village. The collection of eight authentic Acadian homes, furnished with period pieces, dates back to 1800. Displays in each building focus on Acadian culture and traditions.

Vermilionville ★ – *300 Fisher Rd., Lafayette. 337-233-1694.*

www.vermilionville.org. Open year-round Tue–Sun 10am–4pm. Closed Mon & major holidays. $8. Set on the banks of Bayou Vermilion, the 23-acre Cajun-Creole heritage park includes 18 colorfully restored and re-created buildings that preserve the folkways of the early Cajuns, who settled near the bayous because the trees at the bayou's edge provided them with lumber, firewood and shade from the searing summer heat. Inside the buildings, costumed artisans demonstrated traditional crafts such as weaving, boat-building and blacksmithing, while Cajun bands perform daily in a large performance hall.

Vermilionville Highlights

• **La Maison Broussard** – This Creole cottage was once home to Acadian exile Amand Broussard, his wife, and their 13 children.

• **La Chapelle** – A reproduction, La Chapelle des Attakapas typifies the Catholic churches found in the area in the mid- to late 18C.

• **La Cabane** – Boat-building, trap making and decoy carving are demonstrated in this replica of an 18C trapper's cabin.

Is It Cajun or Is It Zydeco?

Only a trained ear can hear the difference between Cajun and Zydeco music. But there is a difference. Zydeco comes from the African-American, French-speaking population of southern Louisiana, while Cajun music is associated with the Canadian exiles' French-speaking white descendants. The main difference between Cajun and zydeco music lies in the use of the fiddle and the accordion: both styles of music use these two instruments, but Cajun relies heavily on the fiddle, while zydeco spotlights the accordion. Both types of music complement their tunes with a washboard, a practice that started with poor but enterprising musicians using what they had on hand in lieu of a purchased source of percussion—Louisiana Cajuns are famous for their ability to turn almost any situation into a good time.

Speaking of good times, get into the spirit of things with a visit to a Cajun dance hall like **Mulate's** *(325 Mills Ave., Breaux Bridge; 337-332-4648; www.mulates.com)* and **Randol's Restaurant & Cajun Dancehall** *(2320 Kaliste Saloom Rd; see Must Eat)* for an introduction to Cajun music and dancing.

Chalmette Battlefield and National Cemetery★

6mi east of New Orleans, in Chalmette. Take Hwy. 46 to 8606 W. St. Bernard Hwy. 504-281-0510. www.nps.gov/jela. Open year-round daily 9am–5pm. Closed Mardi Gras day & Dec 25.

The final battle ever fought between Britain and America was staged on these grounds. Known as the Battle of New Orleans, the confrontation that made a national hero of Andrew Jackson turned out to be moot. Two weeks before the battle took place, the Treaty of Ghent was signed in Belgium, ending the War of 1812. But in the early 19C, news took weeks to cross the Atlantic, so neither General Sir Edward Pakenham, the commander of the British forces, nor Andrew Jackson, who was defending New Orleans, had gotten wind of the treaty when 10,000 British soldiers set out to take the city.

On January 8, 1815, Pakenham ordered 5,400 of his men to attack Jackson's forces, who had retreated to a strategic position behind the banks of the Rodriguez Canal. Hemmed in by the Mississippi River on one side and a cypress swamp on the other, the Brits charged across a clear-cut sugar cane field, only to be mown down by Jackson's men. Fighting lasted less than two hours, at the end of which some 2,000 British soldiers lay wounded or dead (including General Pakenham, who died in the battle). The Americans reported only 13 casualties.

Visit – Begin at the visitor center by viewing the excellent 30-minute video that details the battle; then drive or walk the 1.5mi road that leads past significant points along the battlefield.

Chalmette National Cemetery

Adjoining the battlefield, Chalmette National Cemetery is the last resting place for some 14,000 Union soldiers who fell during the Civil War, including African American Buffalo Soldiers.

Algiers Point

Lying on the opposite side of the Mississippi River from the Central Business District, Algiers Point is a quiet suburb of New Orleans and home to some of the area's best-preserved Victorian and Creole cottages.

How do you get there? Take the ferry. In continuous operation since 1826, the Canal Street Ferry runs from the terminal at the foot of Canal Street across the river to Algiers Point. It's used mainly by commuters, but the 10-minute (one-way) ride affords a splendid view of New Orleans. Try taking the trip at sunset for a romantic—and free—excursion that promises to be memorable. Ferries run daily every 15 minutes from 6am until midnight *(504-565-5451; www.algierspoint.org; cars pay $1 round-trip, pedestrians ride free)*. Don't forget your camera!

Mississippi Gulf Coast★

Visitor information: Mississippi Gulf Coast Convention & Visitors Bureau, 228-896-6699 or 888-467-4853; www.gulfcoast.org.

Ah, the lure of white sands and gentle ocean waves. Fringing the Gulf of Mexico from New Orleans east to Mobile, Alabama, and beyond, the Gulf Coast has long been a haven for sun worshippers, sportsmen, history buffs and more recently, gamblers. Here you'll find antebellum homes, cultural museums, more than 20 golf courses and some 60 charter-fishing operators, as well as a dozen casinos. Of course, the resort communities of Gulf Shores, Pascagoula, Biloxi, Ocean Springs and Gulfport continue to attract visitors to their sandy beaches, warm gulf waters and moderate year-round temperatures.

Mobile★

146mi east of New Orleans via I-10 East. Visitor information: Mobile Convention & Visitors Corporation, 251-208-2000 or 800-566-2453; www.mobile.org.

Mobile's ties to New Orleans are more than geographic. Alabama's second-largest city was the capital of French Louisiana from 1711 to 1719, and its Mardi Gras celebration (the first known festivity took place in 1703) pre-dates the better-known festivities in the Crescent City. Modern-day Mobile combines vestiges of its antebellum past with the bustle of a contemporary southern metropolis. Its prime location at the head of Mobile Bay made the city a major Confederate port during the Civil War, and one of the last Southern cities to fall under Union control. Still a busy port, Mobile is adding to its maritime allure as it completes its new cruise terminal and becomes a permanent home port for the Carnival cruise ship line in October 2004.

Local maps and information are available at the visitor center downtown in **Fort Conde**, a reconstructed version of the early 18C outpost *(150 S. Royal St.; 334-434-7304; www.mobile.org; open year-round daily 8am–5pm; closed Mardi Gras day & Dec 25).*

Dauphin Street Historic District

Mobile's long history dates back to its founding by the French in 1702. One of the main avenues in the new settlement was Dauphin Street, named for the son of Louis XIV. Still a thriving commercial thoroughfare, Dauphin Street and the adjacent blocks are lined with restaurants and shops. Although a fire in 1839 destroyed the 18C wooden buildings here, Dauphin Street claims an impressive array of historic structures, ranging in style from Italianate to Victorian to Art Deco. *To obtain a historic district walking-tour brochure, contact the Mobile Convention & Visitors Corporation (above) or www.mainstreetmobile.org.*

Bellingrath Gardens and Home★★

12401 Bellingrath Rd., Theodore, AL. 334-973-2217. www.bellingrath.org. Grounds open year-round daily 8am–dusk. House tours 9am–5pm (hours vary seasonally). Closed Dec 25. $9 (gardens only). Combination tickets are available for house tours and river cruises.

Bellingrath Gardens' 65 acres bloom year-round with azaleas, roses, hibiscus, chrysanthemums, camellias and poinsettias. Located about 20mi south of Mobile, the land now occupied by the gardens was a fish camp when soft-drink magnate Walter Bellingrath (Mobile's first Coca-Cola bottler) purchased it as a place to relax in 1917. Bellingrath's wife, Bessie, soon filled the grounds with azaleas and camellias. After a trip to Europe in 1927, the couple hired Mobile architect George B. Rogers to turn their rural retreat into a landscaped country estate. The results were spectacular; Rogers added fountains, pools and waterfalls, along with a rock garden and acres of bright azaleas. In spring 1932 the Bellingraths opened their gardens to the public, who came in droves to see the display of azaleas. This enthusiastic public response prompted the opening of the property on a permanent basis.

Gardens – Paved pathways lace the acres of foliage and flowers, passing through the **Rose Garden**, which showcases 75 different varieties, and the **Rockery**, framed by banks of pink azaleas in spring. For a look at less formal flora, follow the quarter-mile raised **boardwalk** through a natural bayou. Visit in December to see the annual Magic Christmas in Lights, when the gardens become a wonderland decked out with 3 million twinkling lights.

Mansion – Built in 1935, Walter and Bessie Bellingrath's 15-room English Renaissance house looks much like it did when they lived there. Rooms are filled with Mrs. Bellingrath's collection of European antique furnishings, porcelain, silver and glassware.

River Cruises

If you haven't had enough nature, take a cruise on the Fowl River. The 150-passenger MV *Southern Belle* departs from the dock at Bellingrath Gardens for a 45-minute sightseeing excursion along the river named for the abundance of osprey, pelicans, blue herons and egrets that frequent its banks and shallows. *For schedules and rates, check online at www.bellingrath.org or www.alabamacruises.com (no sightseeing cruises in Dec & Jan).*

USS Alabama at Battleship Memorial Park★★

2703 Battleship Pkwy. Take I-10 East to Exit 27 (US-90/Battleship Pkwy.). 251-433-2703 or 800-426-4929. www.ussalabama.com. Open Apr–Sept daily 8am–6pm. Rest of the year daily 8am–4pm. Closed Dec 25. $10.

Kids love exploring the many levels of this massive South Dakota-class battleship, built in the Norfolk, Virginia Navy Yard. Launched in 1942, the Alabama served in both the Atlantic and Pacific theaters of World War II; she earned nine battle stars shooting down 22 enemy planes and participating in six land bombardments. The self-guided tour leads you up and down through the multiple decks, which you access via narrow ladder-like stairways.

Other attractions in the park include the World War II submarine USS *Drum*, and a hangar full of historic aircraft, including a B-52 Stratofortress and an A-12 "Blackbird" spyplane.

Fast Facts: USS Alabama

- Length: 680 feet
- Weight: 35,000 tons (under battle conditions, she weighed 42,500 tons)
- Her normal crew was 2,500 men

Gulf Coast Exploreum Museum of Science★

65 Government St. 334-208-6873. www.exploreum.net. Open Mar–mid-Aug Mon–Sat 10am–5pm, Sun noon–5pm. Rest of the year Tue–Fri 9am–4pm, Sat 10am–4pm (hours vary seasonally). $7.75 (combination tickets available for museum and IMAX theater.

Popular with the elementary-school set, the 8,500sq ft Hands-On Hall of inter-active physics both entertains and educates visitors. It's a virtual world at the new Minds-On Hall, where you can create your own fish tank, choreograph your own chorus line on a computer, or play "mad scientist" at the Ciba Lab.

Saucy Q Bar BQ

1252 Government St. 251-433-7427. www.saucyqbarbque.com. Closed Sun.

"Cook 'em til they done" is the motto emblazoned on T-shirts at this family-owned Mobile rib joint, where locals pack the red-vinyl booths at lunchtime. They come for plates piled high with ribs, chicken, pork, beef, smoked sausage and pit-smoked ham, smothered in a special-recipe sauce handed down from the owner's grandmother. Sides of baked beans, coleslaw or potato salad make a fitting—and ample—accompa-niment. Grab a roll of paper towels and join the crowd.

Mobile Museum of Art★

4850 Museum Dr., in Langan Park. Take I-65 North to Springhill Ave. (Exit 5); turn left on Springhill Ave. and continue 1.5mi to John D. New St. Turn left on New St. and right on Museum Dr. 251-208-5200. www.mobilemuseumofart.com. Open year-round Mon–Sat 10am–5pm, Sun 1pm–5pm. $10.

Opened in 2002, Mobile Museum of Art's new building sits in the city's largest public park and includes 95,000sq ft of exhibit space to show off pieces from its permanent collection of more than 6,000 objects. The museum is especially strong in **American art** of the 1930s and 40s and contemporary **American crafts**, but it also includes works from Europe, Asia and Africa. Paintings from the permanent collection dominate the first floor; the second floor displays the museum's holdings of contemporary American crafts and includes space for major traveling exhibits.

Museum of Mobile★

111 S. Royal St. 334-208-7569. www.museumofmobile.com. Open year-round Mon–Sat 9am–5pm, Sun 1pm–5pm. Closed major holidays. $5.

Housed in the 1857 Public Market building, the museum illustrates the story of Mobile from colonization to the present with two floors of displays drawn from its collection of 85,000 artifacts, which includes photographs, documents, portraits, Mardi Gras memorabilia, and a 14C dugout canoe found in Mobile. In the atrium lobby stands "Marianne," the French goddess of Liberty, which once topped the Mobile County Courthouse. Don't miss the display of fine 18C and 19C silver.

Fairhope★

17mi east of Mobile. Take I-10 east to Exit 35, then south on US-98 to US-98A.

From downtown Mobile, it's an easy drive to Fairhope, Alabama, which lies on the eastern shore of Mobile Bay. This idyllic small town boasts sweeping bay views and a colorful main street, **Fairhope Avenue**. A shopper's paradise, Fairhope claims more than 80 retailers, including specialty boutiques, antique shops, art galleries, bookstores and restaurants, along Fairhope Avenue and its adjacent blocks. Head down the hill to find the town's lovely **bayfront park**; just beyond, the municipal **pier** makes the perfect spot to watch the sun set.

Biloxi

93mi east of New Orleans. Take I-10 east to I-110, then south into Biloxi.

This coastal Mississippi city, 61mi west of Mobile, teems with activity from its resorts, fishing port, seafood canneries and boatyards, all blessings of its water-bound location on a peninsula between Biloxi Bay and the Mississippi Sound. Founded in 1699, Biloxi has grown into one of the most popular resorts on the Gulf Coast. Enormous casinos now punctuate the miles of gleaming white beach along Biloxi's shorefront, and charming homes line the residential stretch of Beach Boulevard, along with hotels and shops.

What Else Is Doing in Biloxi?

- **Maritime and Seafood Industry Museum** relates the colorful story of Biloxi's economic mainstay *(115 First St.; 228-435-6320; www.maritimemuseum.org; open year-round Mon–Sat 9am–4:30pm; $5).*

- Check out the sharks, eels, sea turtles and other gulf denizens in the 42,000-gallon Gulf of Mexico tank at the **J.L. Scott Marine Education Center and Aquarium** *(115 Beach Blvd.; 228-374-5550; www.usm.edu/aquarium; open year-round Mon–Sat 9am–4pm; $5).*

Beauvoir★

2244 Beach Blvd., Biloxi. 228-388-1313 or 800-570-3818. www.beauvoir.org. Open Mar–Oct daily 9am–5pm. Rest of the year daily 9am–4pm. $7.50.

President of the Confederate States of America, **Jefferson Davis** (1808–1889), spent the final year of his life in this raised Creole-style cottage on the Mississippi Sound. He was invited here to write his memoirs by the Dorsey family, who owned the house. Opened as a museum in 1941, Beauvoir contains many Davis family furnishings. Displays in the site's **Presidential Library**★ tell the story of Davis' tumultuous life.

Ocean Springs★

1mi east of Biloxi via US-90. Visitor information: 228-497-9934 or www.oceansprings-ms.com. The historic L&N train depot now houses the visitor center: 1000 Washington Ave. 228-875-4424.

A waterside artists' colony, Ocean Springs, Mississippi invites relaxing strolls along pleasant sidewalks lined with antique shops, pottery studios, art galleries and cafes. Be sure to stop in **Shearwater Pottery** *(102 Shearwater Dr.; 228-875-7320; www.walteringlisanderson.com/shearwater.html).* Founded in 1928 by Peter Anderson, the studio now showcases works by members of the Anderson family.

The venues listed below were selected for their ambience, location and/or value for money. Rates indicate the average cost of an appetizer, an entrée and a dessert for one person (not including tax, gratuity or beverages). Most restaurants are open daily and accept major credit cards. Call for information regarding reservations, dress code and opening hours. Restaurants listed are located in New Orleans unless otherwise noted. For a complete listing of restaurants mentioned in this guide, see Index.

$$$$ over $50	**$$ $15–$30**
$$$ $30–$50	**$ less than $15**

Luxury

The Besh Steakhouse $$$$ American

4 Canal St., in Harrah's Casino. No lunch on weekdays. 504-533-6111. www.harrahs.com.

Local culinary star chef John Besh raises the steaks at this handsome beef house housed in a former poker parlor. Featuring an open kitchen, a brandy and cobalt color scheme and a collection of Blue Dog paintings by George Rodrigue, Besh Steakhouse delivers Prime aged beef, including a hefty 30oz. cowboy steak, a buttery flatiron of American kobe, and a dazzling assortment of iced fresh seafood—all big-ticket items. Ask to see the "diamond menu" geared to high rollers with a taste for Petrossian caviar.

Commander's Palace $$$$ Louisiana

1403 Washington Ave. 504-899-8221. www.commanderspalace.com.

The green and white signature awning beckons at this must-eat restaurant, housed in a beautiful Victorian mansion in the Garden District. Both Emeril Lagasse and Paul Prudhomme started here, and the Brennan family has maintained a tradition of culinary excellence with stand-out menu items such as turtle soup laced with sherry, and shrimp remoulade "moderne," layers of Gulf shrimp, crisp greens, shrimp mousse and spicy remoulade sauce. Go for the jazz brunch if you're in town on Sunday.

Emeril's
$$$$ Louisiana

800 Tchoupitoulas St. 504-528-9393. www.emerils.com.

It's been more than a decade since the culinary king of "Bam!" opened his own restaurant in this renovated warehouse space after earning raves in the Commander's Palace kitchen. Although Emeril's often traveling, his culinary style still marks the menu here, from the signature use of his own blend of spices (as in the citrus- and tea-glazed duck) to reinvented comfort food (BLT salad with organic tomatoes). If you like to watch, reserve one of the seats at the kitchen counter for the best view in the house.

Emeril's Delmonico
$$$$ Continental

1300 St. Charles Ave. 504-525-4937. www.emerils.com.

Another Emeril's? You bet! Emeril created quite a splash when he took over this longstanding institution on the edge of the Garden District, poured millions into a sophisticated renovation and transformed a tired space into one of the city's swankiest eateries. Portions are mammoth—try the 20oz Delmonico with marchand de vin sauce, the sautéed rainbow trout with rock shrimp, or the ultra-rich crabmeat Imperial. Save room for the classic bananas Foster, prepared tableside, of course.

Peristyle
$$$$ French

1041 Dumaine St. 504-593-9535.

Chef/owner Anne Kearney has been turning out bold, fresh Louisiana-scented French cuisine for more than a dozen years, and her menu just keeps getting better. Try Gulf shrimp amandine, thyme- and garlic-marinated loin of lamb, or tuna à la Anne, a hearty portion of yellowfin served with potato-celeriac mash and a demi-glace reduction. The restaurant is as popular as it is small, so be sure to make reservations well in advance.

Stella! $$$$ International

1032 Chartres St. 504-587-0091. www.restaurantstella.com.

The hotel dining room decor may be uninspired, but the food will impress at this restaurant named for Stanley Kowalski's bellow in *A Streetcar Named Desire*. Chef Scott Boswell uses Louisiana ingredients in such globally accented dishes as tandoori-spiced Atlantic salmon, tomato-curry purée with cumin-grilled shrimp and cayenne-cured pork loin. The well-thought-out wine list complements the chef's impassioned execution.

Victor's Grill $$$$ French-Creole

921 Canal St., in the Ritz Carlton hotel. 504-524-1331. www.ritzcarlton.com.

This ornate gilded restaurant in the Ritz-Carlton may be a throwback to hotel dining rooms of days gone by, but the updated Creole-American menu is anything but old-fashioned. Garlicky escargots are served in a red wine sauce; and the duck and wild mushroom gumbo is a marriage made in heaven. Order the lobster Victor's and you'll get an oversized Maine lobster brimming with crab meat and artichoke stuffing. For dessert, try the white-chocolate baked Alaska, flamed with New Orleans rum.

Moderate

Antoine's $$$ French-Creole

713 St. Louis St. 504-581-4422. www.antoines.com.

It doesn't get any more traditional than at this French Quarter landmark, which dates back to 1840. The 15 formal dining rooms—and yes, jackets are required—include the Rex Room, all a-glitter with crowns, scepters and Mardi Gras memorabilia. Oysters Rockefeller originated here, and you really should try them, but the fried oysters on buttered toast with foie gras are equally hard to resist. Rich sauces, incredible alligator bisque and pompano en papillote (fish baked in a paper bag) are all signature items. Don't miss the cherries jubilee, flamed tableside.

August $$$ New American

301 Tchoupitoulas St. 504-299-9777. www.rest-august.com.

August spotlights John Besh's Creole-influenced contemporary cuisine in a former grocer's warehouse space now aglow with French doors, red leather chairs and chandeliers. Besh keeps one foot in his native bayou and the other in the big city, putting out creative fare like his BLT—buster crabs, lettuce and heirloom tomatoes—and Louisiana rabbit with morels served with sage grits. The boutique wine list with its 400-plus entries made *Food & Wine's* Best New Wine list in 2002.

Bayona

$$$ International

430 Dauphine St. 504-525-4455. www.bayona.com.

Chef/owner Susan Spicer mines the global table without backsliding into fusion territory—and the results are delicious. Entrées, which change seasonally, travel from the Mediterranean to Asia, India and the Southwest, including seared ceviche with peppered fruit salsa and ancho-mango coulis, grilled duck breast with pepper jelly, and sweetbreads with sherry-mustard butter. The sunny Creole cottage includes a lush plant-filled courtyard.

Brennan's

$$$ Louisiana

417 Royal St. 504-525-9711. www.brennansneworleans.com.

This may be the only restaurant in America where breakfast begins with cocktails, includes an appetizer and ends in dessert, a three-hour process that will surely spoil your appetite for dinner, unless you eat at midnight. Touristy, yes, but that's because it's so much fun. Try the eggs Sardou, poached and served on artichoke bottoms and creamed spinach. Bananas foster is a must—legend has it the flambéed bananas and ice cream dessert was invented here.

Cobalt

$$$ New American

333 St. Charles Ave. 504-565-5595. www.cobaltrestaurant.com.

The most stylish of Susan Spicer's eateries features live jazz and a glitzy bar scene, along with her signature regional American cuisine, such as Grand Central oyster pan roast, Chinatown five-spice duck, seafood enchiladas, and a North Beach antipasto platter. The vibe is sophisticated, so dress to impress. At $10, the lunch specials are a great deal.

Dickie Brennan's Steakhouse

$$$ American

716 Iberville St. 504-522-2467. www.dickiebrennanssteakhouse.com.

Aged USDA Prime beef is the specialty at Dickie Brennan's. Cuts begin at a modest 8oz filet and go up to a 24oz rib eye that can satisfy the heftiest appetite. Blackened prime rib is pan-seared and served on a sour-cream-new-potato mash; the house filet is topped with masa-coated flash-fried oysters and béarnaise sauce. Of course, there are a few non-beef dishes on the menu, but why bother? If you're feeling adventurous, start with the turtle soup—it's a local favorite.

Galatoire's

$$$ French-Creole

209 Bourbon St. 504-525-2021. www.galatoires.com.

New Orleanians are not only loyal to this traditional bastion of Creole dining, they're loyal to their waiter, and if they're old enough, to their waiter's son. Generations come and go, but Galatoire's, with its classic menu of trout meunière, shrimp remoulade, and stuffed eggplant, will never change. If you only choose one French-Creole restaurant, make it this one. Jackets required.

Gautreau's $$$ French-Creole

1728 Soniat St. 504-899-7397.

This tiny, uptown favorite, originally a neighborhood drug store, is a small, elegant space now commandeered by chef Mathias Wolf, whose complex, intense dishes include duck confit with flageolets and red-onion marmalade, rack of veal with braised veal cheeks, and snapper with gnocchi and truffle beurre blanc.

Herbsaint $$$ French

701 St. Charles Ave. 504-524-4114. www.herbsaint.com.

Talented chef Donald Link has officially taken over for owner Susan Spicer at this understated bistro, a perfect backdrop for Link's gutsy, flavorful Franco-American menu. Rooted in down-home sensibility, his dishes—fricasséed rabbit with home-made pappardelle pasta and wild mushrooms; muscovy duck leg confit with dirty rice; Spanish-inspired shrimp with romesco sauce—are all divine.

Indigo $$$ Creole

2285 Bayou Rd. 504-947-0123. www.indigonola.com.

Indigo's Creole cottage ambience is cozy and elegant, with candlelight, plantation windows and a covered patio overlooking the garden. Chef Kevin's contemporary, eclectic Creole cuisine is worth the cab fare to Mid-City. Try dishes like cold smoked catfish with a golden osetra caviar remoulade, crawfish boil vichyssoise, and sautéed wild-mushroom-dusted mangrove snapper.

K-Paul's Louisiana Kitchen $$$ Cajun

416 Chartres St. 504-524-7394 www.chefpaul.com.

Paul Prudhomme, the bigger-than-life father of blackened everything, still lends his interpretation of Acadian cooking to K-Pauls, the best place in town for crayfish and alligator, served with sauce picante when the weather gets nippy. Gumbo is always a good choice here, and so is the blackened yellowfin tuna and sweet-potato pecan pie. Opt for dinner over lunch unless you're up for communal seating.

La Cote Brasserie $$$ French

700 Tchoupitoulas St. 504-613-2350.

Chef René Bajeux oversees this sophisticated seafood restaurant, with its sleek marble bar, wraparound windows, and bustling open kitchen. Here, French bistro seafood meets homey New World Creole and Cajun-influenced dishes, like crispy skewered shrimp on a vegetable-pear slaw, pan-fried redfish with cornbread Johnnycake, and a sweet pork loin chop served with molasses-spiked sweet potatoes.

Marisol
$$$ International

437 Esplanade Ave. 504-943-1912. www.marisolrestaurant.com.

Chef/owner Peter Vazquez put this charming Faubourg Marigny bistro on the N'Awlins culinary map with bold, globally inspired creations like seared Hudson Valley foie gras, steamed mussels and a fiery Thai crab and coconut soup. Fish entrées like the pan-seared pompano with peeky-toe crab salad are outstanding. Save room for the key lime pie, or, if you're not up for sweets, Marisol offers an extensive list of imported cheeses. Weather permitting, snag a table in the tropical courtyard.

Mr. B's Bistro
$$$ Creole

201 Royal St. 504-523-2078. www.mrbsbistro.com.

This sleek bistro, owned by Ralph and Cindy Brennan (Commander's Palace, Palace Cafe, Bacco) is noted for its hickory-grilled steak and seafood, as well as Creole favorites like jambalaya, made with andouille sausage, duck, and chicken and served with spinach fettuccine instead of rice. It's hard to decide between the warm bread pudding soaked in Irish whiskey, and Mr. B's rich mousse cake topped with chocolate ganache.

Muriel's
$$$ Louisiana

801 Chartres St. 504-568-1885. www.muriels.com

This former 18C residence of Jean Baptiste Destrehan was renovated into an intimate series of Victorian dining rooms and bars, complete with the decadent Séance Lounge, supposedly home to a high-spirited spirit. A large menu of regional favorites includes a sampler of crawfish étoufée, seafood gumbo and jambalaya, pecan-crusted puppy drum fish and wood-grilled barbecue shrimp.

Nola
$$$ New American

534 St. Louis St. 504-522-6652. www.emerils.com.

Sporting the city's acronym (New Orleans, LA), this perennial hot spot is the French Quarter digs of celebrity chef Emeril Lagasse. Specialties here include Louisiana crab cakes with Creole tartar sauce, cedar-plank-roasted red fish,

and homemade chorizo and double-cut pork chops with pecan-glazed sweet potatoes. And what would a trip to one of Emeril's restaurants be without tasting one of the sinfully rich desserts? Forget about sorbet and go straight for the white-chocolate bananas Foster bread pudding. Dine at the food bar for a front-row view of the action.

Upperline $$$ Creole

1413 Upperline St. 504-891-9822. www.upperline.com.

Owner JoAnn Clevenger makes everyone feel right at home at her cozy uptown restaurant, located in a restored 19C home filled with local art. Fried green tomatoes with shrimp remoulade, bronzed Mississippi catfish with barbecued crawfish, and watercress and Stilton salad typify some of the fine fare produced by chef Ken Smith. Regulars go for the restaurant's "famous" roast duck with your choice of garlic-port or ginger-peach sauce.

Budget

Acme Oyster House $$ Seafood

724 Iberville St. 504-522-5973. www.acmeoyster.com.

This down-home old-timer, with its scarred marble bar and colorful shuckers, has been an institution forever. Belly up to the bar find out why—briny Gulf Coast oysters, gumbo, po-boys and crawfish étoufée do the trick. Or if you prefer your oysters cooked, go for the oyster loaf, a 12-inch hunk of French bread loaded with fried oysters, dressed with melted butter and pickles. If you find yourself lakeside, drop into Acme's Lakeshore Drive location—there's an outdoor patio and a view of Lake Pontchartrain *(7306 Lakeshore Dr.; 504-282-9200).*

Bon Ton Cafe $$ Cajun

401 Magazine St. Closed weekends. 504-524-3386.

Owned by the Pierce family since it was established in 1953, the Bon Ton dishes up authentic Cajun fare in a c.1840s building in the Central Business District. The restaurant is known for its crawfish, and they serve this tasty crustacean in crawfish étoufée, crawfish Newburg and crawfish jambalaya—or order the crawfish dinner and sample all three. Save room for the bread pudding with whiskey sauce, which consistently wins raves.

Jacques-Imo's Café $$ Creole

8324 Oak St. 504-861-0886. www.jacquesimoscafe.com.

Locals dominate at this foodie destination, where they happily wait for a chance to taste chef-owner Jacques Leonardi's Creole soul food, which has only gotten better since he brought in celebrated local chef Austin Leslie to cook by his side. The place is a gem of a joint—the bar is downright raucous—but you won't find better fried chicken and shrimp-and-alligator-sausage cheesecake anywhere in town.

La Crêpe Nanou
$$ French

1410 Robert St. Dinner only. 504-899-2670.

Behind the velvet maroon curtains of this uptown bistro's doorway is a rustic, casual dining room with vivid original painting of Garden District street scenes. On the menu: peppery escargot baked in butter, and crêpes stuffed with everything from crab and spinach to crawfish or ratatouille. Reservations are not accepted, so be prepared to wait in line.

Lemon Grass
$$ Vietnamese

217 Camp St. 504-523-1200. www.lemongrassrest.com.

Celebrated local chef Minh Bui creates sophisticated French/Vietnamese cuisine, using the freshest of local ingredients and Louisiana seafood and plenty of robust flavors. Try the spring rolls, Vietnamese bird's nest (sautéed scallops and shrimp with Oriental veggies in a crispy potato nest), summer rolls with shrimp and pork, and Asian curried Gulf shrimp. The dining room's light-filled feng shui ambience is almost as refreshing as the kitchen's cuisine.

Lulu's
$$ American

907 Exchange Alley. 504-525-2600. www.lulusinthegarden.com.

Find your way up this pedestrians-only alley and you're in for a treat. Chef/owner Corbin Evans, formerly of Bayona, ups the gastronomic ante with straightforward soups, salads and sand- wiches. Try the local citrus, roasted beet and fennel salad with sprouts and farmer's cheese, or more sophisticated dishes like oxtail gravy with herb gnocchi, and herb- and spice-crusted tilapia with lobster mashed potatoes. Bring your own wine.

Petunia's
$$ Cajun

817 St. Louis St. 504-522-6440. www.petuniasrestaurant.com.

Set in a three-story 19C Creole town house, replete with intricate cypress millwork and original coal-burning fireplaces, Petunia's is the place for hearty breakfasts of savory crêpes, boudin and Cajun sausage, stuffed omelettes and grillades (smothered veal) with gravy over grits. Po-boys, soups and salads make way for a dinner menu that includes fried seafood platters, backfin lump crab- meat and shrimp au gratin, and Cajun pasta with shrimp and andouille sausage.

Santa Fe
$$ Southwestern

801 Frenchmen St. 504-944-6854.

Casual elegance prevails at this South of the Border cantina, with the emphasis on fresh local ingredients incorporated into Southwestern specialties. Go beyond the usual fajitas and tamales and try the seafood combination of crawfish, crab and shrimp enchiladas, chiles rellenos and chalupas. Beware of the potent margaritas, but you'll get almost as high on the chocolate-coconut pecan pie.

Uglesich's
$$ Louisiana

1238 Baronne St. Lunch only. 504-523-8571. www.uglesichs.com.

Locals love this uptown dive and why not? Since 1924 Anthony Uglesich has been delivering the juiciest fried soft-shell crab in the city and a litany of Cajun-Creole specialties that include gumbo thick with shrimp, crawfish and okra, an outstanding oyster po-boy, and bar-b-que shrimp, bathed in olive oil, butter, garlic and parsley. Wash it all down with a spicy bloody Mary. By the way, it's pronounced YOU-gla-sitch-es.

Wasabi
$$ Japanese

900 Frenchmen St. 504-943-9433. www.wasabirestaurant.com.

When you need a break from cream and butter, head over to the funky off-Quarter Faubourg Marigny neighborhood, where international cuisine is everywhere. Wasabi, with its Zen aesthetic and classic neighborhood barroom vibe, is a breath of fresh air. Sushi, special rolls, udon, teriyaki—it's all here, and it's all good.

Bluebird Cafe
$ American

3625 Prytania St. Open until 3pm daily. 504-895-7166.

Breakfast is the favored meal here. The Bluebird's huevos rancheros are locally renowned and the pecan waffles are guaranteed to get you that carb load and then some—but, oh, what a way to go. Locals pack the place on weekends, so go early or be prepared to stand in line.

Central Grocery $ Deli

923 Decatur St. 504-523-1620.

The Tusa family has owned this wonderfully cluttered Italian grocery since 1904, home to the original muffuletta, a Dagwood-sized feast of Italian meats, cheeses and aromatic spicy olive salad. For vegetarians, there's a meatless version, sans salami, etc., that's also delicious. And don't forget to take home a jar of Central Grocery's yummy olive salad for your foodie friends.

Elizabeth's $ American

601 Gallier St. 504-944-9272. www.elizabeths-restaurant.com.

It might not look like much from the outside, but this Bywater favorite delivers its promise of "real food, done real good." Oversized plates of comfort food satisfy both local tradesman and tourists for breakfast and lunch, with menu items from po-boys, gumbo and fried chicken to an amazing duck hash made from chopped duck meat sautéed with onions and green pepper. Prices are rock bottom and everything is tasty.

Fiorella's Café $ American

1136 Decatur St. 504-528-9566.

Cheap eats, salty service, tacky decor—no wonder the locals want to keep this place to themselves. What's the draw? You won't believe how good the fried chicken is, ditto the fried pickles, washed down with a cold beer.

Liuzza's by the Track $ Louisiana

1518 N. Lopez St. 504-943-8667.

You won't find a better corner pub, and you won't taste a better gumbo—although the oyster po-boys with garlic butter and the beef po-boys with mayonnaise and horseradish go down mighty fine with a cold mug of Abita amber ale. Just a block from the Fair Grounds Race Course, this is *the* meeting place for jazz fest attendees who swear by Liuzza's eye-popping spicy bloody Marys.

Mona's Cafe
$ Middle Eastern

504 Frenchmen St. 504-949-4115.

This casual neighborhood cafe in Faubourg Marigny attracts a younger crowd in search of cheap, healthful cuisine and vegetarian options. Stellar choices include garlicky hummus, juicy kabobs, tabouli, baby lamb chops and falafel.

Mother's
$ Louisiana

401 Poydras St. 504-523-9656.

Arguably the best place in town for po-boys, Mother's serves oversize sand-wiches best ordered "dressed"—that is, with the works. Try the house-roasted ham, the soft-shell crab or the fried oysters, and while you're at it, be sure to get a side of fries.

Port of Call
$ American

38 Esplanade Ave. 504-523-0120. www.portofcallneworleans.com.

The best burger in town. That's the main reason to hit this grungy hot spot, with its faux nautical decor and perpetual waiting line. Burgers are char-grilled and come with a baked potato topped with everything from cheese and sour cream to mushrooms. There are other items on the menu—pizza, steak, salad—but most people just go for a burger washed down with a Monsoon, Port of Call's version of Brennan's famous Hurricane cocktail.

Dining in Cajun Country

Prejean's
$$$ Cajun

3480 I-49 North, Lafayette. 318-896-3247. www.prejeans.com.

Nightly Cajun bands and award-winning cuisine draw residents and visiting dignitaries alike. Catfish Catahoula (stuffed with crawfish, crab and shrimp), Rocky Mountain mixed grill (elk, deer and buffalo), and smoked duck and andouille gumbo are among the best-sellers at this northern Lafayette restau-rant. "Big Al," a 14ft-long gator captured in nearby Grand Chenier swamp, presides over the dining room.

Blue Dog Café
$$ Cajun

1211 W. Pinhook Rd., Lafayette. 337-237-0005. www.bluedogcafe.net.

As much a gallery as a restaurant, this cozy cafe has walls covered with some 150 works by local son George Rodrigue, whose Blue Dog is a Loui-siana icon. Specialties include rabbit tenderloin with cheese dipping sauce, a Caesar salad topped with fried shrimp or oysters, corn and crab bisque, and fried and blackened seafood platters. Live jazz is featured on the weekend.

Randol's Restaurant & Cajun Dancehall
$ Cajun

2320 Kaliste Saloom Rd., Lafayette. 337-981-7080. www.randols.com.

A Cajun menu of fried soft-shell crabs, crawfish Caesar salad, thick seafood gumbo, and blackened rib-eye steak brings the crowds in, but it's the music that keeps them here. Randol's Acadian dance hall is a cultural experience not to be missed, with families young and old making time on the dance floor to live music seven days a week.

Dining along the North Shore

Alex Patout's Louisiana Restaurant
$$$ Creole/Cajun

2025 Lakeshore Dr., Mandeville. 985-626-8500. www.patout.com.

Bayou-born chef Alex Patout combines Cajun and Creole specialties at his New Orleans location and now at his restaurant in Mandeville, a two-story 19C French Colonial cottage built for city founder Bernard de Marigny de Mandeville. Devastated by a fire in 2002 (a seafood boiler was left on after closing), the restaurant was completely restored by Patout and architect Lynn Mitchell, down to the finest historic detail. Enjoy a lakefront view on the balcony, while dining on creations like Louisiana wontons, duck and oyster gumbo, and rabbit sauce piquant.

Etoile
$$ French

407 S. Columbia St., Covington. 985-892-4578.

Co-owned by painter James Michalopoulos, this Covington bistro features whimsical decor, a stylish wine bar and gourmet shop, and a menu of specialties like sweet-potato French fries, steamed mussels in a fresh dill and white-wine cream sauce, and grilled tilapia with citrus-herb butter sauce.

Shady Brady's
$$ Southern

301 Lafitte St. Madisonville. 985-727-5580.

Chef Christopher Brady, the creative force behind the wildly successful VooDoo Barbecue in New Orleans, and his wife, Liberty, opened this funky eatery in 2003. Located in a small

cottage just a few blocks off the lakefront, the friendly place specializes in Southern fare, including ribs, overstuffed po-boys, chicken fried chicken, corn pudding and collard greens. Try the Café Buzz for dessert—crème brûlée flavored with ground espresso beans.

The properties listed below were selected for their ambience, location and/or value for money. Prices reflect the average cost for a standard double room for two people (not including applicable city or state taxes). Hotels in New Orleans constantly offer special discount packages. Price ranges quoted do not reflect the city's hotel tax of 13% or the occupancy fee ($1–$3/night). Note that during Mardi Gras, hotel prices can as much as double from their normal rates. Properties are located in New Orleans, unless otherwise specified.

$$$$$	over $300	$$	$75–$125
$$$$	$200–$300	$	less than $75
$$$	$125–$200		

Luxury

Maison Orleans
$$$$$ 75 rooms

904 Iberville St. 504-670-2900 or 800-241-3333. www.ritzcarlton.com.

If you've always wanted a personal butler, you've come to the right place. You'll have access to your own butler 24 hours a day at this opulent hotel, which serves as the concierge level of the adjacent Ritz Carlton. Luxury does come at a high price, but once you're tucked in your room with its Frette linens, down duvets and pillows, hardwood floors, CD/DVD players with surround sound, and oversized marble baths with deep soaking tubs, you'll agree it's worth the splurge. There's even a 20,000sq ft day spa and fitness center on-site. Now that's Southern comfort.

Windsor Court
$$$$$ 324 rooms

300 Gravier St. 504-523-6000 or 888-596-0955. www.windsorcourthotel.com

This luxe property in the Central Business District features $7 million worth of British art and antiques throughout, all keeping with its "House of Windsor" theme. The majority of elegant rooms, done in traditional English style with a private balcony or bay window, are lavish one and two-bedroom suites. When you're not sleeping, an Olympic-size swimming pool, sundeck and large fitness room beckons, and the renowned **Grill Room** restaurant (**$$$$**) tempts with fine regional cuisine.

Bienville House $$$$ 83 rooms

320 Decatur St. 504-529-2345 or 800-535-7836. www.bienvillehouse.com.

Built within the shell of a 19C warehouse, this small hotel boasts amenities not always found in the French Quarter, including handicapped accessibility, four sundecks, a pool, valet parking, and rooms wired for high-speed Internet access. Ask for a room with a balcony, and you'll get a view of either Decatur Street and the river, or a pretty garden courtyard.

Chateau Sonesta Hotel New Orleans $$$$ 251 rooms

800 Iberville St. 504-586-0800 or 800-766-3782. www.chateausonesta.com.

Ideally situated on the border between the French Quarter and the Central Business District, the building now occupied by Chateau Sonesta opened in 1849 as a department store. Front rooms have large windows facing Canal Street (perfect for watching Mardi Gras parades); others have balconies overlooking Bourbon or Dauphine streets. Individually designed guest rooms boast 12ft ceilings and interesting configurations, with nooks and crannies adding architectural appeal. Guests can charge dinner at nearby Red Fish Grill to their rooms.

Fairmont Hotel $$$$ 700 rooms

123 Baronne St. 504-529-7111 or 800-527-4727. www.fairmont.com.

This legendary grande dame, once a favorite of infamous ex-governor Huey Long, was the model for Arthur Hailey's novel *Hotel*. Dating from 1893 and visited by a litany of presidents and glittering stars, the Fairmont's opulent block-long lobby (it runs from Baronne Street to University Place in the Central Business District) looks its best when decked out in holiday finery. Rooms are spacious, and outfitted with amenities like down pillows and large marble or tile baths. Named for its signature cocktail, the hotel's **Sazerac Bar** is one of the city's most popular watering holes *(see Musts for Fun).*

Hotel Maison de Ville $$$$ 23 rooms

727 Toulouse St. 504-561-5858 or 800-634-1600. www.maisondeville.com.

This two-story c.1800 town house, with its antique furniture, plush Oriental rugs and serene colors, seems a world away from Bourbon Street. Choose among luxurious accommodations in the town house, the former slave quarters, the carriage house, and in the seven small, self-contained Audubon Cottages. Although they're each different in decor, all rooms have feather beds, Frette linens and mini bars. Literature fans will want to know that Tennessee Williams lived in room number nine, where he worked on *A Streetcar Named Desire.*

Le Pavillon Hotel $$$$ 226 rooms

833 Poydras St. 504-581-3111 or 800-535-9095. www.lepavillon.com.

This hotel's sumptuous gilt lobby, with its Italian marble and grand chandeliers, is a local landmark in the Central Business District. Some of the art-filled guest rooms are small, but there are antiques throughout and a beautiful rooftop swimming pool to stave off the swampy summer heat. In an unusual hotel tradition, peanut butter and jelly sandwiches and cold milk are offered as a late-night buffet.

Loews New Orleans Hotel $$$$ 285 rooms

300 Poydras St. 504-595-3300 or 800-235-6397. www.loewshotels.com.

The newly opened Loews has transformed a former office building into a 21-story luxe hotel, complete with the Brennan family-run Café Adelaide (named for colorful Ti Adelaide Martin, co-owner of Commander's Palace) and the Swizzle Stick Bar, that honors Adelaide's favorite accoutrement. Large rooms boast endless amenities, from city and river views to laptop-size safes to high-speed Internet access, and local art on the walls. The Romanesque Piazza d'Italia behind the hotel is being restored to its former glory for outdoor special events.

Loft 523 $$$$ 18 rooms

523 Gravier St. 504-200-6523. www.loft523.com.

This urbanely hip hotel is housed in a 19C warehouse in the Central Business District, allowing for 12ft ceilings in all 18 spacious rooms. Guest quarters are Soho-style lofts with massive wooden beams, stark spotlighting, Sony CD/DVD systems, and fabulous Italian marble baths (dual showerheads encourage romance). The two penthouses have garden terraces, and one is even equipped with a plasma screen television. Warm and fuzzy, it's not, but for those in search of chic urban appeal, this is the spot.

Renaissance Arts Hotel

$$$$ 217 rooms

700 Tchoupitoulas St. 504-613-2330 or 888-236-2427. www.marriott.com.

The brick exterior and high ceilings of this four-story former warehouse (1910) attest to its industrial roots. Opened in 2003 in the burgeoning Warehouse District, just a half-mile from the Aquarium of the Americas, the hotel incorporates dramatic art including sculptures by Dale Chihuly, Lyn Emery, and others. The building wraps around a glass-topped atrium/sculpture garden, making space for spacious well-appointed rooms. A fitness center and outdoor swimming pool are located on the roof.

Ritz-Carlton

$$$$ 452 rooms

921 Canal St. 504-524-1331 or 800-241-3333. www.ritzcarlton.com.

Located in a gorgeous Beaux-Arts building that formerly housed the legendary Maison Blanche department store, the Ritz-Carlton is a luxurious haven of gracious hospitality, with amenities including a state-of-the-art spa *(see Must Be Pampered)*, the popular French Quarter Bar for jazz, and a club-level lounge with a terrific city view. Rooms are outfitted with feather beds, down comforters and silky 300-thread-count Frette linens. **Victor's Grill ($$$)** has recently relaxed its jackets-required dress code as well as its menu.

Royal Sonesta Hotel

$$$$ 500 rooms

300 Bourbon St. 504-586-0300 or 800-766-3782. www.sonesta.com.

Step inside this busy, crossroads hotel and enjoy attentive service, a myriad of bars, restaurants and shops, and amenities like a fitness facility and a heated outdoor pool. Rooms are furnished with antique reproductions; many offer French doors and wrought-iron balconies that overlook either a garden courtyard or noisy Bourbon Street—the latter not conducive to sleep. Guests on the private seventh-floor tower level have access to extra perks such as a separate concierge, and complimentary continental breakfast and evening hors-d'oeuvres.

Soniat House

$$$$ 33 rooms

1133 Chartres St. 504-522-0570 or 800-544-8808. www.soniathouse.com.

A short walk from the Café du Monde, this classic set of three Creole-style town houses in the residential French Quarter haven't changed much since they were built in the 1830s. Spiral staircases lead to rooms decorated with European and Louisiana antiques and hand-carved canopy beds wrapped in fine fabrics and Egyptian cotton sheets. Don't miss breakfast by the lily pond in the charming courtyard.

W Hotel $$$$ 98 rooms

316 Chartres St. 504-581-1200, 888-625-5144. www.whotels.com.

This small hotel, formerly Hotel de la Poste, was recently purchased and redone by the swank New York chain. Sleek styling and minimalist decor is a W trademark, but very different for the French Quarter. Contemporary-style chambers may be small, but the beds are piled high with down pillows and comforters, and rooms are equipped with 27-inch color TVs. Have a difficult question? The hotel's "whatever/whenever" service caters to guests' most eccentric whims.

Moderate

Bourbon Orleans Hotel $$$ 211 rooms

717 Orleans St. 504-523-2222. www.bourbonorleans.com.

The glittering Orleans ballroom, once home to Quadroon Balls, a mingling of Creole gentlemen and mixed-race women, forms the centerpiece of this stately hotel in the heart of the French Quarter. With its Oriental rugs and crystal chandeliers, the peach and cream lobby sets the stage for gracious guest rooms sporting marble baths and Queen Anne-style furnishings. If you want a good night's sleep, make sure your room doesn't face Bourbon Street.

Degas House Bed & Breakfast $$$ 7 rooms

2306 Esplanade Ave. 504-821-5009 or 800-755-6730. www.degashouse.com.

Home to French Impressionist painter Edgar Degas from October 1872 to April 1873, this restored 1852 home boasts 14ft ceilings and polished hardwood floors. Antiques, period reproduction pieces, and Degas prints decorate the rooms. Guests are served a complimentary continental breakfast in the room believed to have been the artist's studio *(see Historic Sites)*.

Hotel Monaco $$$ 250 rooms

333 St. Charles Ave. 504-561-0100 or 866-685-8359. www.monaco-neworleans.com.

The Kimpton group favors historic buildings for its Monaco properties, and the New Orleans version is no exception. A 1926 Masonic temple with its elaborately tiled barrel-vaulted entranceway ceiling forms the shell for this artsy hotel in the Central Business District. Whimsical decor features zebra prints in

the lobby, pistachio-green walls in the guest rooms, black granite in the bathrooms and faux mink throws on the bed. If you get lonely, you just have to ask and they'll put a goldfish in your room to keep you company (or you can bring your own pet). Basketball players take note: the Monaco offers "tall rooms" with 9ft-long king beds and heightened shower heads.

Hotel Provincial

$$$ 94 rooms

1024 Chartres St. 504-581-4995 or 800-535-7922.
www.hotelprovincial.com.

This family owned hotel caters to a business clientele with data ports in every room, on-site parking and meeting rooms. Listed on the National Register of Historic Places, the hotel is actually a complex of restored town houses, slave quarters and commercial buildings offering guest quarters outfitted with Creole antiques and French reproductions. For breakfast, be sure to try the yummy beignets at the hotel's cafe.

Hubbard Mansion

$$$ 5 suites, 2 apartments

3535 St. Charles Ave. 504-897-3535. www.hubbardmansion.com

The Hubbard's Garden District location is ideal for watching Mardis Gras, since one of the parades passes right outside the door. This elegant Greek Revival mansion is full of heirloom antiques and gracious hospitality. Rooms open onto a central hallway, which leads to the dining room, where owners and longtime New Orleans residents Rose and Don Hubbard serve a tasty continental breakfast each morning.

International House

$$$ 119 rooms

221 Camp St. 504-553-9550 or 800-633-5770. www.ihhotel.com.

Just across Canal Street from the French Quarter, International House was built in 1906 as the world's first international trade center (hence the name). This boutique hotel boasts artisan furniture and a calm, modern sensibility. Rooms are large and simply designed in neutral tones with Aveda products and brushed aluminum fixtures in the bathrooms. Loa, the casual lounge off the lobby, is named for a voodoo priestess.

Hotel Le Cirque

$$$ 137 rooms

936 St. Charles Ave. 504-962-0900 or 800-684-9525.
www.hotellecirqueneworleans.com.

Set on the edge of the trendy Warehouse Arts District, Le Cirque transformed a former YMCA hostel into a stylish, minimalist hotel decorated with black-and-white photographs and contemporary art. Room amenities include sleek, modern design details, spacious baths and extra comfy beds. Lee Circle Restaurant takes up most of the ground floor. The St. Charles streetcar runs right outside the front door.

Le Richelieu $$$ 86 rooms

1234 Chartres St. 504-529-2492 or 800-535-9653. www.lerichelieuhotel.com.

Set on the edge of the French Quarter, Le Richelieu is reminiscent of an up-scale 1970s motel. In fact, not much has changed since Paul McCartney lived in one of the suites for two months in 1977 while recording an album. Despite the lack of frills, rooms are comfortable, the staff is friendly, and there's a small outdoor pool and courtyard. The price includes free self-parking on the premises—the only hotel in the Quarter offering that amenity.

The Monteleone $$$ 573 rooms

214 Royal St. 504-523-3341 or 800-535-9595. www.hotelmonteleone.com.

Owned by the Monteleone family for four generations, the hotel has grown from a 14-room lodging in 1886 to today's 16-story building with its signature Baroque granite façade, ceiling frescos and ornate chandeliers. In keeping with its French Quarter location, the vibe is European, from the bustling lobby to the well-appointed guest rooms and suites. The hotel recently completed a $60-million renovation, refurbishing its rooms with earth-toned fabrics and new marble and granite bathrooms.

Budget

Baronne Plaza Hotel $$ 181 rooms

201 Baronne St. 504-522-0083 or 888-756-0083. www.baronneplaza.com.

This restored 1931 Art Deco gem, just a block from Canal Street and the French Quarter, offers oversize rooms, a snazzy marble lobby (the floors are original), and a workout room. Honeymoon suites are equipped with Jacuzzi tubs, a fridge and a microwave. Valet parking and airport shuttle service are available for an extra fee.

Chateau Hotel $$ 45 rooms

1001 Chartres St. 504-524-9636. www.chateauhotel.com.

Personal service is a hallmark of this modest hotel, with its friendly courtyard bar and simple but comfortable rooms, some of which boast exposed brick and wood beams along with king-size four-posters or painted iron beds. Others are decorated in traditional furnishings. Be sure to ask for room with a full-size bathtub—not all of them are. A swimming pool and free valet parking are extra perks.

Chimes Bed & Breakfast $$ 5 suites

1146 Constantinople St. 504-488-4640 or 800-729-4640. www.chimesbandb.com.

Owner Jill Abbyad runs this renovated 1876 cottage like it was her own home—in fact, she and her family live in the main house across a brick courtyard from the guest suites. Individually decorated guest quarters may feature four-poster beds, claw-foot tubs, and handmade lace curtains; each room has a private bath and a courtyard entrance. And the property is located just a short walk from St. Charles Avenue and Magazine Street.

Cornstalk Hotel $$ 14 rooms

915 Royal St. 504-523-1515 or 800-759-6112. www.travelguides.com/home/cornstalk.

The Cornstalk takes its name from the ornate cornstalk and morning glory design on its cast-iron fence. Former owner Dr. Joseph Biamenti built the fence as a gift to his wife in 1850, since she was homesick for the Midwest. Some of the rooms are tiny, but all are furnished with antiques and include private baths. The hotel's spacious porch overlooks Royal Street.

Frenchmen Hotel $$ 27 rooms

417 Frenchmen St. 504-948-2166 or 800-831-1781. www.frenchmenhotel.com.

One of the few hotels in the Marigny neighborhood, these two adjoining 1850s town houses offer a prime location on the edge of the French Quarter and steps away from the happening Faubourg Marigny restaurant and bar scene. Rooms are dark and utilitarian, but rates include continental breakfast, and there's a small courtyard pool and Jacuzzi.

Prince Conti Hotel $$ 71 rooms

830 Conti St. 504-529-4172 or 800-366-2743. www.princecontihotel.com.

Antique-filled rooms (some with smallish baths), the Bombay Club restaurant, and a friendly, helpful staff—many of who have been with the hotel for years—are a few reasons why you'll like this European-style pension. A reno-vated town house, dating back to 1829, is available for private functions and special events.

Ursuline Guest House $$ 13 rooms

708 Ursulines St. 504-525-8509 or 800-654-2351.

This gay-friendly guesthouse offers a pleasant courtyard with hot tub, complimentary wine each evening, and comfortable, modest rooms. Pastry and coffee are served in the courtyard each morning. Ask about reserving a parking space—availability is limited. Guests here must be 18 years of age and older.

Staying along the North Shore

Annadele's Plantation
$$$ 4 rooms

71495 Chestnut St., Covington. 985-809-7669. www.annadeles.com.

 Located on the banks of the Bogue Falaya River in down-
town Covington, this lovely restored plantation boasts the
first-class **Annadele's Plantation restaurant ($$$)**, with
chef Pat Gallagher in the kitchen turning out top-notch
New Orleans-style cuisine. Rooms are full of Southern
charm and antiques, with views of the manicured grounds,
moss-draped oaks and swimming pool. Both king- and
queen-size beds are available.

Garden Guest House B&B
$$$ 2 suites

34514 Bayou Liberty Rd., Slidell. 985-641-0335 or 888-255-0335. www.gardenbb.com.

Convenient to tours of Honey Island Swamp, this homey B&B sits on 10 acres
of bayou, woodland and gardens. Run by Bonnie and Paul Taliancich, who live
in a cottage on the property, Garden Guest House is known for its outstanding
breakfasts—Bonnie's buttermilk biscuits are legendary—and its well-appointed
quarters. Each guest suite has its own private entrance, fireplace and deck, and
sleeps up to eight guests. The living room of each spacious accommodation
boasts floor-to-ceiling windows with garden views.

Little River Bluffs—A Nature Preserve
and Retreat
$$$ 3 cabins

11030 Garden Lane, Folsom. 985-796-5257. www.littleriverbluffs.com.

Ideal for nature lovers, these secluded cabins
in the 50-acre Little River Bluffs section of
the Folsom forest offer peace and serenity.
Each cabin has a view of the sandy banks of
the Tchefuncte River and of the hardwood
forest, home to magnolia, cypress, white oak
and pine trees. Marked trails are great for
amblings and bird-watching, and the river is
perfect for kayaking and tubing. Private decks,
hot tubs, fireplaces and a stocked larder number among the amenities. Two of
the cabins even have cable TV, in case you don't want to be too far from civili-
zation. The Bluffs are about an hour outside of New Orleans.

Mar Villa Guest House
$$ 2 rooms

2013 Claiborne St., Mandeville. 985-626-5975. www.marvilla.com.

Just one mile from Lake Pontchartrain, this comfortable guest house in Old
Mandeville is within walking distance of local restaurants, Tammany Trace bike
path and the North Star Theatre. The former boarding house is beautifully
restored, featuring original pine floors, beaded-wood ceilings and an inviting
veranda. Rooms have private entrances and baths, as well as refrigerators.

Staying in Cajun Country

Aaah! T'Frere's Bed & Breakfast $$ 6 rooms

1905 Verot School Rd., Lafayette. 337-984-9347 or 800-984-9347. www.tfreres.com.

Built in 1880 of Louisiana red cypress hauled from the nearby Vermilion Bayou, this cozy inn includes a porch for dining, a full Cajun-style breakfast and of course, mint juleps served out on the veranda. Rooms are appointed with Louisiana antiques, including the 1800 Mallard bed, the centerpiece of the Mary room. The hearty Cajun breakfast includes eggs, spicy smoked sausage, and crêpes topped with sugar-cane syrup.

Bois des Chenes B&B $$ 5 rooms

338 N. Sterling St., Lafayette. 337-233-7816. www.boisdeschenes.com.

Located in a historic 1820 plantation house and listed on the National Register of Historic Places, this Acadian style plantation house is filled with Louisiana antiques and collectibles. All of the rooms are spacious, with three located in what used to be the carriage house behind the main property. Amenities include cable TV, refrigerators, and one room has a wood-burning fireplace. Host Coerte Voorhies speaks French.

Lafayette Hilton $$ 327 rooms

1521 W. Pinhook Rd., Lafayette. 337-235-6111 or 800-774-1500. www.Lafayette.Hilton.com.

Located less than two miles from the center of downtown Lafayette, this newly refurbished full-service chain hotel offers standard but comfortable rooms with high-speed Internet access, a restaurant and lounge, and a fitness center. If you request a room in the VIP tower, you'll also get a complimentary continental breakfast and evening hors-d'oeuvres.

Index

Index

Index

Photo Credits

Beth d'Addono 32, 48; Alex Patout's Louisiana Restaurant 113; Annadele's Plantation 122; Antoine's 104; Arthur Roger Gallery 27; Beauregard-Keyes House & Garden 33; Belladonna Spa 86; Blue Dog Café 112; Chateau Sonesta Hotel 115; Contemporary Arts Center 53; Peter Dobczynski 49, 77; Degas House 4, 38, 118; Elizabeth's 111; Emeril's 103, 107; Fairmont Hotel New Orleans 39; Hermann-Grima/ Gallier Historic Houses 34, 40; Hilton Hotels 123; Historic New Orleans Collection 46; Historic Urban Plans 20; ©Robert Holmes 18-19; Indigo 106; International House 119; Kimpton Group 118.

Louisiana Office of Tourism: 5, 6, 7, 21, 25, 29, 30, 31, 34, 35, 45, 47, 50, 58, 59, 61, 62, 64, 67, 68, 69, 71, 73, 76, 77, 78, 80, 90, 91, 93, 94, 95, 96, 106, 119.

Lafayette Convention and Visitors Commission 92, 123; Le Chat Noir 82; Le Cirque Hotel 119; Little River Bluffs—A Nature Preserve and Retreat 122; Louisiana Landmarks Society 41; Louisiana State Museum 4, 36, 55; Lulu's 109; Mignon Faget 79; Mobile Area CVB 97, 98, 99; Mother's 112; Mr. B's Bistro 107; Musée Conti Wax Museum 49; Museum of Mobile, Steve Groaum 100; MICHELIN: Gwen Cannon 101.

New Orleans Metropolitan CVB: 56; Romney Caruso 60; Harry Costner 3, 8, 9; Jack Edwards 78; Richard Nowitz 6, 8, 9, 23, 24, 37, 40, 42, 61, 66, 76, 108; Ann Purcell 8, 22, 25, 26, 43; Carl Purcell 4, 63.

NewOrleansOnline.com: 43, 105, 108, 116, 117, 120; Ron Calamia 81, 117; Troy Gomez 57; Michael Terranova 9, 22, 28.

New Orleans City Park: Romney 70, Michael Terranova 44; New Orleans Museum of Art, Judy Cooper 51; New Orleans Northshore: ©Jeff Greenberg 64-65 (icon), 65; New Orleans Pharmacy Museum 54; Oak Alley Plantation 5, 88, 91; Odgen Museum of Southern Art 52; Orpheum Theater 74; Rosemary Parrillo 111; Petunia's 109; Praline Connection Gospel Hall 84; Ritz-Carlton Hotel 87, 104, 114-115, 117; Rock-N-Bowl 83; Royal Street Inn 85; Saenger Theatre 75; Schroeder Hotels 117; Shadows-on-the-Teche, National Trust Historic Site 93; Shady Brady's 113; ©2001 SimoneInk 102-103, 116; Six Flags New Orleans 72; Starwood Hotels & Resorts Worldwide 118; Uglesich's 110; Ursuline Guest House 121; Wasabi 110.

Cover photos:
Front Cover: ©Lemass/FOLIO, Inc.; Front Cover small left: Carl Purcell, New Orleans CVB; Front Cover small right: Ann Purcell, New Orleans CVB; Back Cover: Jeff Strout, New Orleans CVB; Inside Back Cover Flap: Base map ©Mapquest.com.

YOUR OPINION MATTERS!

Thank you for purchasing a Michelin travel publications product. To help us continue to offer you the absolute best in travel guides, maps and atlases, we need your feedback.

Please fill in this questionnaire and return it to:
Michelin Travel Publications – Attn: Marketing
P.O. Box 19001
Greenville, SC 29602-9001, USA

To thank you, we will draw one name from the returned questionnaires each month from May 2004 to year end. Each month's winner will receive a free 2004 North America Road Atlas, or a set of the Must SEES travel guides, or a set of the Regional Road Atlas + Travel Guides.

1. How would you rate the following features of the product, if applicable?
1 = *Very Good*   **2** = *Acceptable*   **3** = *Poor*

	1	2	3
Selection of attractions/sights	❏	❏	❏
Practical Information (prices, etc.)	❏	❏	❏
Description of establishments	❏	❏	❏
General presentation	❏	❏	❏
Cover	❏	❏	❏

2. How satisfied were you with this product?

❏ Very satisfied   ❏ Satisfied   ❏ Somewhat Satisfied   ❏ Not Satisfied

If not satisfied, how should we improve the product? _____

_____

3. Did you buy this product: *(check all that apply)*
   ❏ For holiday/vacation
   ❏ For short breaks or weekends
   ❏ For business purposes
   ❏ As a gift
   ❏ Other

4. Where would you buy and expect our products to be available?
   (check all that apply)

   ❏ Supermarket   ❏ Mass Merchandiser (Costco, Sam's, etc.)
   ❏ Convenience store   ❏ Specialty store (museum shop, travel store, etc.)
   ❏ Bookstore   ❏ Gas/Service Station
   ❏ Online   ❏ Kiosk/Gift shop

5. Which destinations do you visit the most often for pleasure? *(list as many locations as you wish)* _____

_____

MSNO04

Tear Here

6. Which destinations do you visit the most often for business? *(list as many locations as you wish)* _____

_____

7. When you go on vacation, generally how long do you stay? *(check all that apply)*
❏ Three or four days
❏ One week
❏ Two weeks
❏ A combination of short (three or four days) and one-week vacations
❏ Other _____

8. When you travel, what mode of transportation do you most frequently use? *(1 - most frequent, 6 - least frequent)*
_____Plane _____Car _____Bus _____Train _____Cruise _____Other

9. Would you consider buying other Michelin travel books or products?

❏ Yes ❏ No

If yes, which one(s):
❏ Must SEES
❏ North America 2004 Road Atlas
❏ North America Regional Road Atlas + Travel Guide
❏ North America Regional Road Atlas
❏ North America Regional Maps
❏ Green Guide (North American titles)
❏ Green Guide (European titles)
❏ Red Guide
❏ European City Maps
❏ Other_____

10. Your age?
❏ Less than 25 years old ❏ 25–35 years old ❏ 36–45 years old
❏ 46–55 years old ❏ 56–65 years old ❏ 65 years plus

11. Additional Comments:

_____

_____

Telephone or e-mail where we may reach you: _____

If you would like to be added to our mailing list, please fill out the information below:

❏ Ms. ❏ Mrs. ❏ Mr.

Name _____

Address _____

City_____ State _____

Zip Code_____ Country_____

E-mail (optional):

_____